英语1单元过关检测

主　编　唐正林
副主编　胡　鑫　王　倩
参　编　李　芳　刘明炤　邹　茜　刘　婷　周文彬
　　　　熊寒春　廖　星　王　端　陈兵武　庞启娟
　　　　杜　晶　高芬远　黄银华　魏春辉　赵立英

版权专有　侵权必究

图书在版编目(CIP)数据

英语1单元过关检测／唐正林主编． -- 北京：北京理工大学出版社，2024.6.
ISBN 978-7-5763-4226-0

Ⅰ．G634.413
中国国家版本馆 CIP 数据核字第 2024S2D645 号

责任编辑：王晓莉　　　文案编辑：王晓莉
责任校对：周瑞红　　　责任印制：施胜娟

出版发行／北京理工大学出版社有限责任公司
社　　址／北京市丰台区四合庄路6号
邮　　编／100070
电　　话／(010) 68914026（教材售后服务热线）
　　　　　(010) 68944437（课件资源服务热线）
网　　址／http://www.bitpress.com.cn
版 印 次／2024年6月第1版第1次印刷
印　　刷／定州启航印刷有限公司
开　　本／889 mm×1194 mm　1/8
印　　张／6.5
字　　数／134千字
定　　价／28.50元

图书出现印装质量问题，请拨打售后服务热线，负责调换

前 言

本书依据《中等职业学校英语课程标准》(2020年版)编写，按照课程标准要求，全面贯彻党的教育方针，践行社会主义核心价值观，落实立德树人根本任务，培育英语学科核心素养；立足中等职业教育实际和学生身心发展规律，进一步激发出学生的英语学习兴趣，使其掌握英语基础知识和基本技能，并为以后的职业生涯和终身发展打下坚实基础。

在编写过程中，我们的设计理念如下：

1. 立足教材，夯实基础知识

本书以教材单元任务为依据，挖掘每个单元的基础知识，紧扣教材编写相应的练习，帮助学生有效学习知识并提高综合能力。

2. 围绕话题，拓展语用能力

本书紧扣教材单元教学话题，编写有效的阅读材料和书面表达任务，提升学生的语篇意识和思维能力，进而增强其阅读能力和语言应用能力。

3. 紧扣课标，提升核心素养

本书坚持以培养学科核心素养为宗旨，兼顾职业特色和价值导向，创设真实情境，引导学生形成正确的价值观。

本书在编写过程中，邀请了众多长期从事中等职业教育教学研究工作的专家和一线职教资深专家参与，内容丰富，题型设计合理，对中等职业学校学生非常实用。但是由于时间有限，难免存在不足之处，恳请广大读者提出宝贵意见和建议，以便于修订完善。

编 者

目 录

Unit 1 单元测试 ………………………………………………… (1-4)

Unit 2 单元测试 ………………………………………………… (1-4)

Unit 3 单元测试 ………………………………………………… (1-4)

Unit 4 单元测试 ………………………………………………… (1-4)

Unit 5 单元测试 ………………………………………………… (1-4)

Unit 6 单元测试 ………………………………………………… (1-4)

Unit 7 单元测试 ………………………………………………… (1-4)

Unit 8 单元测试 ………………………………………………… (1-4)

期中检测题 ……………………………………………………… (1-6)

期末检测题 ……………………………………………………… (1-6)

参考答案 ………………………………………………………… (1-6)

Unit 1 单元测试

一、根据首字母或中文意思完成句子。(5小题，每题1分)

1. His name is Jim Green, so his f_____ name is Green.
2. John is a m_____ and he is very busy every day.
3. The students are _____(精力充沛的), because they often play basketball after school.
4. I like sports very much, e_____ playing basketball.
5. Bob lives in the _____(社区) and it is very beautiful.

二、从方框中选择正确的短语并用正确的形式填空。(5小题，每题2分)

cook   introduce   visit   be strict with   vocational

6. Tom works as a teacher in a _____ school.
7. My parents _____ us, especially my father.
8. His grandma lives alone in her own house and he often _____ her on weekends.
9. Hello, everyone, let me _____ a new classmate to you.
10. My father is a chef and he likes _____.

三、单项选择。(10小题，每题1分)

11. Tom _____ France.
    A. come from   B. from   C. is from   D. is

12. Chinese people put _____ name before given name.
    A. first   B. family   C. given   D. give

13. My younger brother is energetic, because he _____ jogging every morning.
    A. goes   B. go   C. went   D. going

14. Light _____ faster than sound.
    A. travel   B. traveling   C. traveled   D. travels

15. In the photo, my father is holding a baby in _____ arms.
    A. he   B. his   C. her   D. hers

16. The children often _____ football on the playground.
    A. play   B. playing   C. plays   D. played

17. _____ you often visit your grandparents?
    A. Did   B. Does   C. Do   D. Are

18. —_____ does your brother do?
    —My brother is a doctor in a hospital.
    A. What   B. Who   C. How   D. When

19. Bill _____ with his parents and younger sister.
    A. live   B. living   C. lived   D. lives

20. He _____ an egg, a glass of milk for breakfast every morning.
    A. have   B. has   C. had   D. having

四、语言应用。(5小题，每题2分)

21. Mary's sister likes _____ according to the picture.

    A. comedy   B. action   C. cartoon

22. How many people are there in the picture?

    A. Five.   B. Six.   C. Seven.

23. From the picture, we know that today is _____.

— 1 —

A. Women's Day   B. Mother's Day   C. Mothers' Day

24. We can know that she is a _____ from the picture.

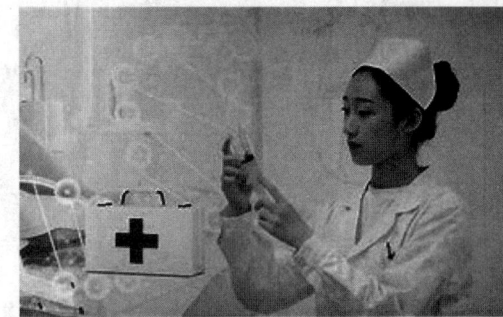

A. teacher   B. driver   C. nurse

25. Who is the man in the picture? He is _____.

A. Zhou Shuren   B. Zhou Jiaosheng   C. Zhou Boyi

五、阅读理解。(15 小题, 每题 2 分)

A

This is a photo that is very special to me. In the photo, there is a beautiful girl who has smiles on her face. She is my sister. The picture was taken on her birthday 14 years ago.

I still remember that was a beautiful day, she was so happy that she even forgot to have breakfast. Because so many friends would come to the party she had prepared for a few days. I made a card by myself as a birthday gift and I took this picture for her.

Although it had passed a long time, we still remember the moment. We're not only sisters but also good friends. I think we'll never forget that unforgettable time.

26. Who is the girl in the photo?
    A. She is my sister.   B. She is a doctor.
    C. She is my mother.   D. She is my teacher.

27. When was this photo taken?
    A. Four years ago.   B. Fourteen years ago.
    C. Forty years ago.   D. Forteen years ago.

28. What did I give to my sister on her birthday?
    A. A book.   B. A Pen.   C. A card.   D. A photo.

29. My sister felt _____ on that day.
    A. sad   B. unhappy   C. sorry   D. happy

30. From the passage, we know the writer _____ her sister.
    A. hate   B. love   C. dislike   D. doesn't

B

Hello, everyone! My full name is Zhang Yunhua. My family name is Zhang and my first name is Yunhua. I'm sixteen years old. My father works in a computer company. He is an engineer. My mother works in a company. She is a busy woman. I have a elder sister and a younger brother. My sister is a student of Hope Vocational School. My brother is a primary school student. He is 8 years old.

I also study in Hope Vocational School. My favorite subject is English, because it is a very useful language to learn. I major in Tourism Service. My dream job is an English tour guide. I want to introduce China to international visitors. It's a perfect job!

I wish to make friends with all of you. You may call me at 15678322468. My e-mail address is 65487932@qq.com.

31. The writer's family name is _____.
    A. Zhang   B. Yun   C. Yunhua   D. Hua

32. There are _____ people in writer's family.
    A. 4   B. 5   C. 6   D. 7

33. The writer's sister is a _____.

A. engineer　　　B. worker　　　C. tour guide　　　D. student

34. The writer's favorite subject is _____.

　　A. Chinese　　　　　　　　　B. English

　　　C. maths　　　　　　　　　D. physics

35. The writer thinks that _____.

　　A. his younger brother is busy　　　B. his mother is lazy

　　C. English is a very useful language　　　D. tour guide is a bad job

C

Sunday, May 14, 2023

Dear Mom and Dad,

　　I'm graduating, and I thank you both for all your help during these 16 years. I still remember when you used to say, "You can be whatever you want." I'm so glad you are my parents, **especially** when I heard some classmates said they didn't get along well with their parents. I'm glad that you are agree with me when I decide to do anything. You always try to help me.

　　Dad, I still remember when you first took me fishing. I also remember when I would cry, you would always be there to try to cheer me up. You are a good father. Sometimes you don't agree with me, but you are there by my side in anything that I do.

　　Mom, I enjoy going out with you and having our happy time every Saturday night, and I hope that never changes. I love telling you everything about my school life. I'm glad we do a lot together. You always give me some useful advice.

　　Thank you for bringing me up.

Love always,

Sam

36. From the text, we can know that Sam is _____ years old this year.

　　A. fifteen　　　　　　　　　B. sixteen

　　C. fourteen　　　　　　　　　D. seventeen

37. The underlined word "especially" in Paragraph 1 means "_____".

　　A. 尤其　　　　　　　　　　B. 专业的

C. 职业的　　　　　　　　　D. 精力充沛的

38. Sam heard some classmates said they _____ their parents.

　　A. liked to listen to　　　　B. had problems with

　　C. liked to talk to　　　　　D. got on well with

39. Who did Sam go fishing with for the first time?

　　A. His mother.　　　　　　B. His classmates.

　　C. His father.　　　　　　D. His parents.

40. Sam writes the letter to show _____ to her parents.

　　A. help　　　　　　　　　B. wishes

　　C. love　　　　　　　　　D. thanks

六、把左右栏相对应的句子匹配起来。（5小题，每题1分）

41. What's your name?	A. I am from China.
42. Nice to meet you.	B. Four.
43. Where are you from?	C. Nice to meet you, too.
44. What's your job, Mary?	D. My name is Linda.
45. How many people are there in your family?	E. I am a nurse.

七、英汉互译。（15小题，每题2分）

46. Let me tell you something about my family.

_____

47. The boy standing next to my father is my little brother.

_____

48. My English teacher often helps me with my English.

_____

49. My father is preparing a handmade plane for my younger sister.

_____

50. The sun rises in the east and sets in the west.

_____

51. Lu is his mother's family name and Xun means being fast.

_____

52. 老师们对我们严格要求，特别是我们的语文老师。

The teachers are _____ us, especially our Chinese teacher.

53. 早上许多老人在公园慢跑。

Many old people _____ in the park in the morning.

54. 他们计划为她举办一个生日派对。

They _____ hold a birthday party for her.

55. 我们应该多注意自己的健康。

We should _____ more _____ to our health.

56. 顺便问一下，你来自哪里？

_____

57. 这个小男孩一定是你。

_____

58. 重阳节快到了。

_____

59. 我们经常乘公共汽车上学。

_____

60. 他独自住在一个大房子里。

_____

Unit 2 单元测试

一、根据首字母或中文意思完成句子。(5 小题，每题 1 分)

1. Many companies h_____ the super stars in order to catch the customers' eyes.
2. A network of railways has spread over the _____（省）.
3. With the popularity of computers, it is c_____ to look up information.
4. Please write your name, a_____ and telephone number.
5. Old people don't like to vary their _____（习惯）.

二、从方框中选择正确的短语并用正确的形式填空。(5 小题，每题 2 分)

| worry about | rush hour | on the right | shuttle bus | be late for |

6. Hurry up, or you'll _____ class.
7. Is there a _____ to the airport that early?
8. Don't _____ the matter, and take it easy.
9. You can see the library _____.
10. I don't think driving is a good choice in the _____.

三、单项选择。(10 小题，每题 1 分)

11. The children are advised to _____ home before dark.
    A. arrive at   B. get to   C. arrive in   D. get
12. Wait until the bus stops before you _____.
    A. get on   B. get off   C. get up   D. get down
13. —Thank you very much.
    —_____.
    A. With pleasure   B. It's a pleasure
    C. It's kind of you   D. Have a good time
14. I used to _____ to school. But now I go to school on foot.
    A. ride a bus   B. by bus   C. take a bus   D. by a bus
15. You'd better _____ if you want to pass the exam.
    A. work hard   B. not work hard
    C. to work hard   D. not to work hard
16. —_____ have you had your toothache?
    —For three days.
    A. How long   B. How soon   C. How far   D. How often
17. It's too late. Please _____ any noise, will you?
    A. not making   B. make   C. not to make   D. don't make
18. After a long way, I feel _____ when I reach the top of the mountain.
    A. tiring   B. interesting   C. tired   D. interested
19. It only _____ 10 minutes to school on foot.
    A. spends   B. costs   C. pays   D. takes
20. Riding a bike is _____ greener than taking a car.
    A. more   B. much more   C. much   D. more much

四、语言应用。(5 小题，每题 2 分)

21. What's the meaning of the sign?

    A. You can go skating on the thin ice.
    B. Watch out because of the thin ice.
    C. It is safe to play on the thick ice.

22. If you want to queue, you should _____.

    A. turn right   B. turn left   C. turn around

23. The owner of this passport comes from _____.

— 1 —

A. The United Nations B. the United Kingdom C. the USA

24. You can _____ to load goods.

A. turn left B. turn right C. go straight

25. The sign means _____ can stop here.

A. all vehicles B. car and bike C. only bus

五、阅读理解。(15 小题，每题 2 分)

A

Cleaning a mountain

At 884,443 meters high, Mount Qomolangma is the tallest mountain on Earth. While it is famous for its beautiful views, parts of the mountain are facing a problem: garbage. Every year, thousands of visitors throw away tons of trash, such as cans and plastic bags.

According to the UN, over 140 tons of trash has been left on the mountain. To reduce trash, China is limiting the number of people who are allowed to climb up the north side of the mountain. Only 300 people will be allowed to climb it, and only during spring, CGTN reported.

Local residents cleaned the mountain last year, removing trash at a height of 5,200 meters.

This year, the local government plans to spend 4 million yuan on a new clean-up campaign. Clean-up workers will also collect the bodies of dead climbers. In 2017, over 280 climbers have died while climbing the mountain, the Paper noted.

The local government is also setting up stations to sort, recycle and break down garbage collected from the mountain. A group of artists will also try to turn the trash into artwork. They will show these works of art locally to remind people not to leave trash when climbing the mountain.

26. The first paragraph mainly discusses _____.
    A. how high Mount Qomolangma is
    B. which the tallest mountain on earth is
    C. why Mount Qomolangma is famous
    D. the problem Mount Qomolangma faces

27. What is China doing to get rid of the trash on Mount Qomolangma?
    A. Stopping people from climbing the mountains.
    B. Limiting the number of climbers.
    C. Asking climbers to bring trash down.
    D. Encouraging people to climb up the south side of the mountain.

28. When can people climb Mount Qomolangma, according to China's new rule?
    A. In spring. B. In summer. C. In autumn. D. In winter.

29. What do we know from the story?
    A. Only 300 people can climb up the north side of Mount Qomolangma every year.
    B. Volunteers around the world did the clean-up on the mountain.
    C. The local government will spend $4 million to clean up the mountain.
    D. An average of 280 climbers die while climbing the mountain every year.

30. Where is the passage probably from?
    A. A fashion magazine.   B. A novel.
    C. A piece of news.   D. A science book.

B

Chengdu Traditional Chinese Medicine Museum
    Location: No 6 Xinchuang Road in Wuhou District
    Ticket: 20 yuan ($3.15)
    Operated by Chengdu University of TCM, Chengdu TCM Museum is the first museum in China to specialize in traditional Chinese medicine. The museum consists of four indoor exhibition halls and two herb gardens.

Chuanju Opera Art Museum

　　Location: No. 8 Cihuitang Street in Jinjiang district

　　Ticket: free

　　Chuanju Opera, a traditional Chinese opera that originated in Sichuan province nearly 1,700 years ago, is a Chinese cultural treasure. The Chuanju Opera Art Museum in Chengdu is the first of its kind in China. The museum has three exhibition halls.

Chengdu Mahjong and Tea Museum

　　Location: No. 1 Baiyunsi Road in Qingyang district

　　Ticket: 100 yuan ($15.81)

　　Chengdu Mahjong and Tea Museum is the world's largest museum about mahjong, a popular traditional Chinese game. Its collections include ancient mahjong sets made of paper, jade and bone. The museum have also more than 400 collections about the tea culture in Sichuan province.

West China Insects Museum

　　Location: No. 2 Qingchengshan Road in Dujiangyan city

　　Ticket: Free

　　Housing nearly 400,000 rare insect samples from 40 countries around the world. The West China Insects Museum has the largest insect collection in Asia.

Teddy Bear Museum

　　Location: Jinma International Sports Center in Wenjiang district

　　Ticket price: 60 yuan ($9.44) for an adult, free for children up to 1.2-meter-tall (one free child per paying adult)

　　The Teddy Bear Museum in Wenjiang is the biggest in its kind in the world. It has 12 themed exhibition halls.

31. Where can we see this picture?

　　A. Science magazine.　　　　　　B. Guide book.

　　C. Tashion handbook.　　　　　　D. Story book.

32. Which museum is the first of its kind in China?

　　A. Teddy Bear Museum.

　　B. West China Insects Museum.

　　C. Chengdu Mahjong and Tea Museum.

　　D. Chengdu Traditional Chinese Medicine Museum.

33. Which museum is the most expensive?

　　A. Chuanju Opera Art Museum.

　　B. West China Insects Museum.

　　C. Chengdu Mahjong and Tea Museum.

　　D. Chengdu Traditional Chinese Medicine Museum.

34. Mr White and Mrs White have three children (height is below 1.2 meters), if the whole family want to visit Teddy Bear Museum, they need to pay _____.

　　A. 120 yuan　　　B. 180 yuan　　　C. 300 yuan　　　D. 60 yuan

35. Which of the following is TRUE according to the information?

　　A. Chuanju Opera Art Museum has nearly 1,700-year history.

　　B. Chengdu Traditional Chinese Medicine Museum has three exhibition halls.

　　C. Chengdu Mahjong and Tea Museum have more than 400 collections about Mahjong.

　　D. West China Insects Museum has 400,000 rare insect samples from all over the world.

C

　　In Ben Elton's book Gridlock, aliens come to our world to learn about people. They look at the places where we live and work, and how we travel. But they don't understand cars. They see that every morning hundreds of millions of people get into big boxes. These boxes take the people many kilometers to their workplace. But often, the big boxes can't move because there are so may of them. Then, in the evening, the people get into their boxes and slowly drive home again.

　　Why don't people travel in the faster boxes they call trains and buses? Or live near their workplace? Do they like to sit in boxes for hours? Or aren't they very smart? It's often because houses are too expensive in the city. People who lived in the city before have to live outside it now. But many jobs are in the city center. Cheaper houses in cities are a possible answer to traffic problems.

　　Bicycles are a good answer, too. They don't make smoke. They're good for our bodies and they're fun. But cycling to work can be hard. Very hard if you live many kilometers from your workplace.

　　Working at home is also good for traffic and people. With computers and the Internet, many people work at home now.

　　36. At the beginning of the passage, the writer leads in the topic by _____.

A. introducing a new movie B. giving examples
C. answering questions D. learning something from aliens

37. The meaning of the underlined word "boxes" in the first paragraph is _____.
   A. bikes B. trains
   C. buses D. cars

38. How many answers to solving traffic jams according to the passage?
   A. One. B. Two.
   C. Three. D. Four.

39. The reason why people don't live near their workplaces is that _____.
   A. they like to sit in vehicles for hours
   B. they are not clever
   C. houses in the city are expensive
   D. they don't want to live near the workplaces

40. The following are advantages of bicycles except that _____.
   A. they don't make smoke
   B. it is hard to ride to work if you live far from your workplace
   C. they are good for our body
   D. they are fun

六、把左右相对应的句子匹配起来。(5小题，每题1分)

41. Could you tell me how to get to the library?	A. I want to try that blue skirt.
42. The math problem is difficult. I can't work it out.	B. Don't worry about it. Let me help you.
43. Why not go shopping with us this afternoon?	C. Go straight and turn left at the third crossing. You can't miss it.
44. What can I do for you?	D. Thank you.
45. Hope everything is all right with you.	E. It's very kind of you.

七、英汉互译。(15小题，每题2分)

46. I don't have too much homework to do this weekend.
   _____

47. It's really one of the driving forces for us to keep going.
   _____

48. You should take the shuttle bus before 9 p.m.
   _____

49. There are many shared bikes at the next bus stop.
   _____

50. I prefer staying at home to going shopping.
   _____

51. Get up early and you can catch the early bus.
   _____

52. 乘地铁去机场大约需要三十分钟。
   It will _____ about thirty minutes to _____ the airport.

53. 到最近的银行要花费我多长时间？
   _____ will it take to get to the nearest bank?

54. 在我们学校附近有一家医院。
   _____ a hospital near our school.

55. 地铁站的对面是一个图书馆。
   The subway station is _____ a library.

56. 沿着这条路直走，在第一个路口右拐。
   _____

57. 你能告诉我去颐和园的路吗？
   _____

58. 在中华站换乘地铁3号线。
   _____

59. 你想乘车还是坐地铁去？
   _____

60. 我正在考虑乘坐出租车。
   _____

Unit 3 单元测试

一、根据首字母或中文意思完成句子。(5小题，每题1分)

1. This new book is about t_____ Chinese culture.
2. More and more people begin to enjoy o_____ shopping.
3. She wrote many _____（畅销的）books.
4. Tom speaks English b_____ than Ben does.
5. This T-shirt is too big. I need a s_____ size.

二、从方框中选择正确的短语并用正确的形式填空。(5小题，每题2分)

on sale   fitting room   pay with   be good for   be rich in

6. Can I _____ my cell phone?
7. Swimming _____ our health.
8. Goji berries _____ vitamins.
9. 150 yuan. They are _____ now.
10. The _____ is over there.

三、单项选择。(10小题，每题1分)

11. — Which is _____, milk or coffee?
    — Milk, I think. I drink it every day.
    A. most delicious　　　　　　B. much delicious
    C. less delicious　　　　　　D. more delicious

12. This place is not big enough for Lucy's birthday party. We should find a _____ one.
    A. bigger　　　B. smaller　　　C. big　　　D. small

13. The writer's new book is not as _____ as her last one.
    A. better　　　B. worse　　　C. good　　　D. bad

14. There _____ 50 boys in my class.
    A. is　　　B. are　　　C. have　　　D. has

15. — This box is too heavy for me to carry. _____?
    — Ok.
    A. Can you help me　　　　　B. What's wrong with you
    C. May I help you　　　　　　D. Pardon me

16. The Summer Palace is one of the _____ places in the world.
    A. Famous　　　　　　B. very famous
    C. more famous　　　　D. most famous

17. It takes me two hours _____ the house.
    A. cleaning　　　B. to clean　　　C. clean　　　D. cleans

18. You shouldn't _____ your hope. Everything will be better.
    A. give out　　　B. give in　　　C. give up　　　D. give away

19. _____ you work, _____ you are.
    A. The hard; the lucky　　　　B. The harder; the lucky
    C. The hard; the luckier　　　D. The harder; the luckier

20. They'd like _____ thank the following people _____ their help and support.
    A. to; to　　　B. for; for　　　C. to; for　　　D. for; to

四、语言应用。(5小题，每题2分)

21. Which sign means "snowy"?

    A. ☁ 　　　B. ☁☀ 　　　C. ☁❄

22. What can we learn from the picture?

    请勿翻越　Please do not climb
    请勿抛物　Plcese do not parabolle

    A. You can climb.　　B. You can't climb.　　C. You can parabolic.

— 1 —

23. We can't _____ in this area.

　　A. enter　　　　B. take photos　　　C. talk

24. In the school days, the drivers need to drive _____.

　　A. less than 40 km/h　　B. more than 40 km/h　　C. 40 km/h

25. You can get the shoes for _____.

　　A. $350　　　　B. $175　　　　C. $150

五、阅读理解。(15 小题，每题 2 分)

A

Project Hope is a volunteer organization offering international and national programs. With all kinds of chances to use your special knowledge to give help, you will be able to improve the lives of those less rich and truly make a difference in this world.

When applying:

Please be ready to submit(提交) your resume(简历) including words explaining why you want to volunteer with Project Hope and be ready to answer a few questions.

What to expect if you have successfully submit your application(申请).

You will receive our e-mail back once we get your application.

Your application will be checked by our headquarters and other offices. Once we accept you, we will call you for an <u>interview</u>. It should take fifteen to twenty minutes. If not, we hope you have a better choice.

If you have any questions, please feel free to e-mail us at volunteers @ projecthope. com.

We look forward to working with you!

26. What kind of organization is Project Hope?
　　A. Sporty.　　　　B. Fee-paying.　　　C. Compensatory.　　D. Voluntary.

27. You need to submit your _____ if you want to join the Project Hope.
　　A. photo　　　　B. bank card　　　C. ID card　　　D. application

28. What does the underlined word "interview" mean?
　　A. 观看　　　　B. 观察　　　C. 面试　　　D. 复试

29. When you have the interview, the whole process (过程) may take about _____.
　　A. seventeen minutes　B. forty minutes　　C. half an hour　　D. an hour

30. If you have any questions, you can _____.
　　A. send e-mails　　B. write letters　　C. call us　　D. come here

B

When you finish some chores at home, will your parents give you a reward(奖励)? It is common for parents to do that. But some people do not think it is a good idea.

One of them is Susie Walton, an education expert. She believes if kids get rewards, they will think that housework is not worth doing unless they get something in return. Kids won't sweep the floor if they see it is dirty. But they will if their parents reward them for it. Walton also says, "A home is a living place for everyone in the family. It's important for kids to see that we all should play our part in keeping our home clean."

Other people don't think so. They believe that rewards encourage kids to do more chores. Rewarding them also teaches them real world lessons. They can learn that they need to work to make money. Now, there are also mobile phone apps like ChoreMonster. With the app, kids get points after doing chores. After getting some points, they can do something they like. For example, parents will allow them to play video games for half an hour if they get 80 points.

So each side seems to have their own reasons. Whether you give children rewards depends on your own ideas. Maybe you have better ways to solve this problem.

31. How many reasons does Susie Walton give in the second paragraph?
   A. One.   B. Two.   C. Three.   D. Four.

32. Which of the following is Susie Walton's opinion?
   A. Don't give kids rewards for doing chores.
   B. Don't ask kids to do housework.
   C. Don't allow kids to play computer games.
   D. Don't let children play a part in doing chores.

33. What do people want to teach kids by giving kids rewards for doing chores?
   A. People need to work to make money.
   B. Doing chores is a good way to make money.
   C. They can only be allowed to watch TV by doing chores.
   D. They must share housework because they live in the same house.

34. What types of this article?
   A. Prose.   B. Essay.   C. Instruction.   D. Narrative.

35. What is the author's attitude in the passage?
   A. Support Susie Walton's opinion
   B. Kids shouldn't offer to help with chores at home.
   C. Apps are better choices for parents than money.
   D. The article doesn't mention

C

Sally didn't know what was wrong with her grandma. She was always forgetting things, like where she put the sugar and what time to have dinner.

"She might have Alzheimer's disease (阿尔茨海默病)," her mother said. "We might have to put her in a nursing home(养老院) so that she can get proper care."

"Oh, that's terrible! She'll miss her own house!" Sally said.

"Maybe, but we can see her on weekends," her mother answered. "We can bring her presents." "Like ice-cream? Grandma loves strawberry ice-cream!" Sally said.

The first time they visited Grandma, Sally wanted to cry. Grandma sat all by herself in the corner of the room. Sally hugged Grandma. "Look!" she said. "We brought you strawberry ice-cream!" Grandma took it and began to eat without saying a word.

"She doesn't seem to know us." Sally was upset. " You have to give her time," her mother said. But the next time it was the same. Grandma ate the ice-cream, but didn't say anything.

"Grandma, do you know who I am?" Sally asked. "You're the girl who brings me the ice-cream," Grandma said. "Yes, but I'm Sally, your granddaughter. Don't you remember me?" "Sure. You're the girl who brings me ice-cream." All of a sudden, Sally realized that Grandma would never remember her.

"Oh, how I love you, Grandma!" she said. Just then she saw a tear roll down Grandma's cheek (脸颊). "Love," she said. "I remember love."

36. What was the matter with Sally's grandma?
   A. She always felt upset.
   B. She ate too much ice-cream.
   C. She always forgot things.
   D. She put more sugar while cooking.

37. What did Sally's grandma do when they visited her first time?
   A. She began to cry.
   B. She began to eat strawberry ice-cream.
   C. She watched others eating strawberry ice-cream.
   D. She sat all by herself in the corner of the room.

38. Did Grandma remember Sally?
   A. No.   B. Yes.   C. Not sure.   D. Maybe.

39. Which statement is TRUE according to the passage?
   A. Sally and her family visited Grandma three times a week.
   B. Sally wouldn't mind whether Grandma can remember her name or not.
   C. Grandma doesn't love strawberry ice-cream anymore.
   D. Grandma will be taken home to get better care.

40. What is the best title for the passage?

A. The Great Power of Hugs.
B. Food Is the Best Medicine.
C. Love Can Always Remain in the Heart.
D. An Introduction to Alzheimer's Disease.

六、把左右栏相对应的句子匹配起来。(5 小题，每题 1 分)

41. What can I do for you?	A. Yes, I'm Amy, a new intern.
42. How much are they?	B. 100 yuan.
43. How long will it take me to get there?	C. I'd like a pair of shoes, please.
44. Are you new here?	D. Nice to meet you, Miss Li.
45. I'd like you to meet my teacher, Miss Li.	E. About thirty minutes.

七、英汉互译。(15 小题，每题 2 分)

46. The Internet is changing the way we shop.

_____

47. Double Eleven is one of the best-known online shopping days in China.

_____

48. More and more people begin to enjoy online shopping.

_____

49. Clothes made of cotton are usually cheaper than those made of silk.

_____

50. How much is three plus one?

_____

51. This kind of book sells well.

_____

52. 让我们试着解开这道数学题。

Let's try to _____ this math problem.

53. 玻璃杯里有多少牛奶？

_____ milk is there in the glass?

54. 这张桌子由木头制成。

The table is _____ wood.

55. 越多越好。

The _____, the _____.

56. 请用英语解释这篇文章。

_____

57. 他写了很多本畅销小说。

_____

58. 良好的沟通很重要。

_____

59. 他比班里的任何一个学生都高。

_____

60. 这张名单上包含许多新名字。

_____

Unit 4　单元测试

一、根据首字母或中文意思完成句子。(5小题,每题1分)

1. The s_____ workers are teaching the students.
2. They plan to h_____ an English competition this week.
3. P_____ makes perfect.(熟能生巧)
4. Going on a school trip is so e_____.
5. What's your f_____ subjects?

二、从方框中选择正确的短语并用正确的形式填空。(5小题,每题2分)

| sound like | different from | be over | all kinds of | take part in |

6. Now, classes _____. You can have a free talk with your friends.
7. In a vocational school, students have _____ after school activities.
8. Vocational high schools are not _____ normal high schools.
9. The story _____ true.
10. To be healthy, you should _____ the sports meeting actively.

三、单项选择。(10小题,每题1分)

11. Look at the black clouds, it _____.
    A. rains　　B. will rain　　C. is going to rain　　D. rained
12. I will choose to go into a vocational school after _____ middle school.
    A. leaving　　B. will leave　　C. leaved　　D. leaves
13. You'll learn some special subjects _____ your major at the vocational school.
    A. relate　　B. related with　　C. related to　　D. relates to
14. _____ fun it is to fly kites on a windy day!
    A. What　　B. How　　C. What an　　D. How a
15. They are _____ the final exam.
    A. prepare for
    B. preparing for
    C. prepares for
    D. preparing with
16. Reading aloud is a great way _____ your English.
    A. to improve　　B. improving　　C. improved　　D. improves
17. There _____ a parents meeting next Monday.
    A. is going to have　　B. is going to be
    C. is going to do　　D. has
18. —Tom, don't be late again. —_____.
    A. Never mind　　B. No, I don't
    C. Sorry. I won't　　D. Sorry. I will
19. Don't _____ too much time on playing games.
    A. pay　　B. spend　　C. cost　　D. have
20. His father will be back _____ 3 weeks.
    A. after　　B. for　　C. with　　D. in

四、语言应用。(5小题,每题2分)

21. The man spent the least money in _____.

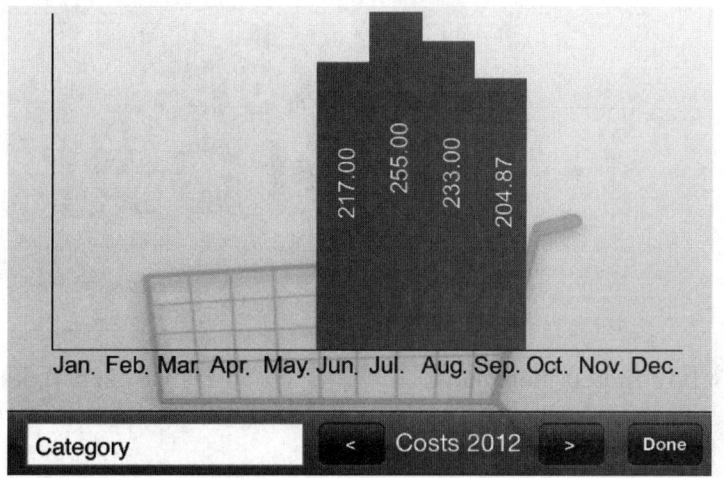

    A. June　　B. August　　C. September

22. The flight will took _____ to arrive at the destination.

    A. 9 hours and 35 minutes
    B. 13 hours and 35 minutes
    C. 14 hours and 25 minutes

— 1 —

23. We should _____ when we see this sign.

A. drive very fast   B. drive slowly

C. stop to take a photo

24. According to the sign, we _____.

A. can't buy tickets here now   B. can sell tickets

C. can get a ticket

25. Which of the following is TRUE according to the information?

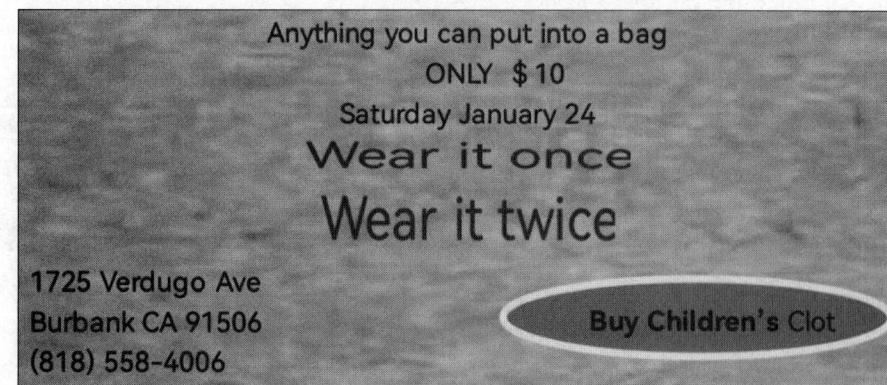

A. You can buy a bag of things for $10 on Jan. 24th.

B. You can buy clothes for your mother here.

C. The shop's telephone number is (818)558-91506.

五、阅读理解。(15小题，每题2分)

A

In many American universities, students should finish thirty-six courses for their degree. A typical course consists of three classes per week for fifteen weeks. A student will attend four or five courses during each semester. It is possible for a student to move between one university and another during his degree course.

The scores of the courses will be recorded, and the record will be shown to their future employers. Students will find a better job if they have good scores. Any student who breaks the rules will appear before a student court. Some students would like to take part in the elections (选举) for entering student organizations. A student who is in student organizations is much respected and it will be of benefit to him later in his career.

26. How many classes does a typical course have for one semester?

A. 3.   B. 15.   C. 20.   D. 45.

27. According to the first paragraph, an American student is allowed to _____.

A. live in a different university

B. live at home and drive to classes

C. get two degrees from two different universities

D. attend four or five courses during each semester

28. Why the scores of the courses will be recorded? Because _____.

A. teachers need the records

B. universities need the records

C. student court needs the records

D. it is useful for students to find a better job

29. Any student who breaks the rules will _____.

A. leave the university   B. apologize to the university

C. appear before a student court   D. be shown to their future employers

30. Some students would like to enter the student organizations because _____.

A. they don't like their study

B. such positions are usually well paid

C. they will be able to stay longer in the university

D. such positions will be of benefit to him later in his career

B

Jack's School Life	I am Jack, a student in Grade 10. I enjoy my school life very much. I have 5 classes in the morning and 3 classes in the afternoon. I study English, Chinese, math and some other subjects. I like Chinese best because it is easy and interesting. I'm not good at math, but I am working hard on it. After class, I often play basketball with my classmates. I go to the school library for some reading twice a week.
Zhang Xin's School Life	My name is Zhang Xin and I am a student at No. 4 Vocational High School. Our school is large and beautiful. I am happy to study here. I usually get to school at 7 o'clock and our morning reading begins at half past seven. I have 7 classes a day, 4 in the morning and 3 in the afternoon. Our last class ends at 4:30 p.m. After that, I spend half an hour doing sports. It is good for my health.

31. How many classes does Jack have every day?

    A. Six   B. Seven

    C. Eight   D. Nine

32. Jack goes to the school library _____.

    A. twice a week   B. twice a month

    C. twice a year   D. twice a day

33. Zhang Xin begins to read in the morning at _____.

    A. at 7:00   B. at 7:30

    C. at 8:00   D. at 9:00

34. What do Jack and Zhang Xin have in common?

    A. They usually do sports.

    B. They have eight classes every day.

    C. They are from vocational schools.

    D. They go to the school library twice a week.

35. Which is WRONG according to the passage?

    A. Jack likes reading.

    B. Jack does not do well in math.

    C. Zhang Xin has four classes in the morning.

    D. Basketball is Zhang Xin's favorite sport.

C

Hello, everyone! Let me ***show you around*** my school. My school is not big, but it's very beautiful. I love my school. There is a broad road in the center of my school. Near the two sides of the road, there are two teaching buildings and a meeting hall.

Around the road, there are some flowers and trees. In spring, we can see many butterflies and other insects. We watch they dance in the flowers. They dance so beautifully. In summer, we can catch grasshoppers among the grass. We have great fun there. On the right side of the road, there is a library and a big playground. There are many kinds of books in the library. After lunch, we often go to the library to read some interesting books. We often read books about animals and interesting stories. We can learn a lot from the books. We do morning exercise every day. In spare time, we often play football and ping pang. Last month, we had a sports meeting. We were all very excited, especially when we saw the teachers' running race.

36. The writer in introducing his _____ to others.

    A. his family   B. his friends

    C. his school and school life   D. his teachers

37. Last month, there was _____ in the author's school.

    A. a sports meeting   B. sports meeting

    C. a parents meeting   D. sport meeting

38. What do they usually do after lunch every day?

    A. Have a good sleep in the classroom.

    B. Play online games on the playground.

    C. Read books in the library.

    D. Do morning exercise on the playground.

39. What's the Chinese for the underline words "***show you around***" in para. 1?

A. 带你参观 B. 给你看一看
C. 围着你走 D. 拿给你看

40. In their free time, they usually _____.
   A. do some sports   B. chat with friends
   C. watch butterflies eat flowers   D. help the teachers run

六、把左右栏相对应的句子匹配起来。(5 小题，每题 1 分)

41. Have a good summer holiday!	A. P. E.
42. Will you have lunch with your roommates?	B. I like it very much.
43. How do you like your school life?	C. Thanks. The same to you.
44. What's your favorite subject, Linda?	D. So he does.
45. Mike likes English very much.	E. Yes. We have planed it before.

七、英汉互译。(15 小题，每题 2 分)

46. I like computer, but it's not my favorite.
_____

47. I think English is useful and interesting.
_____

48. Shall we go together after school?
_____

49. Where are they going to have a picnic tomorrow?
_____

50. I can prepare for the meeting after finishing the work report.
_____

51. Having fun can help us relax and help us learn.
_____

52. 在学校，你可以参加各种各样的活动。
You can _____ all kinds of activities.

53. 我们会后为运动会做演示。
We will _____ a presentation _____ the sports meeting.

54. 我们团队打算明天下午讨论新产品的发展计划。
Our team is discussing the _____ plan for the _____ tomorrow afternoon.

55. 职业学校的学生需要特别注意实践训练。
Vocational school students need to _____ to practice training.

56. 你不应该花太多时间玩网络游戏。
_____

57. 听起来职业高中和普通高中没有差别。
_____

58. 去工厂实习是学好技能的好办法。
_____

59. 明年我将从光华职业学校毕业。
_____

60. 7月6号到10号我们将举行期末考试。
_____

Unit 5 单元测试

一、根据首字母或中文意思完成句子。(5小题，每题1分)

1. I want to invite you to a welcome b_____ tomorrow evening.
2. We look f_____ to seeing you at this celebration.
3. Can you give us some _____(建议)for the party activities?
4. Your support has played an important r_____ in our company's growth.
5. I can h_____ with the preparation.

二、从方框中选择正确的短语并用正确的形式填空。(5小题，每题2分)

help with　　in common　　opening ceremony　　on behalf of　　play an important role in

6. Tom went to the business trip _____ his company.
7. I will be invited to attend the _____ of the new shop tomorrow.
8. Now, smart phones _____ our daily life.
9. Her sister always _____ her Math.
10. What do the Spring Festival and Christmas have _____?

三、单项选择。(10小题，每题1分)

11. We _____ enough food and drinks for the celebration.
    A. buy　　　　B. have bought　　　　C. has　　　　D. has bought
12. My parents aren't at home. They _____ to my uncle's birthday party.
    A. goes　　　　B. went　　　　C. have gone　　　　D. has gone
13. _____ a welcome party for the new students next Saturday.
    A. There is
    B. There was
    C. There is going to be
    D. There has
14. Su Bingtian _____ a sportsman.
    A. is well-known as
    B. was famous for
    C. is famous
    D. is well-known for
15. We want to _____ this opportunity to thank you.
    A. support　　　　B. attend　　　　C. give　　　　D. take
16. They have been friends _____.
    A. in 2020　　　　B. last year　　　　C. since 2020　　　　D. this year
17. He _____ the car for 2 years.
    A. buys　　　　B. has bought　　　　C. has kept　　　　D. keeps
18. —How long has her grandmother been _____? —For 20 years.
    A. dead　　　　B. died　　　　C. die　　　　D. dies
19. Li Xiaonian _____ pay 50 yuan for the lost library book.
    A. must　　　　B. have to　　　　C. has to　　　　D. can
20. When _____ Lucy _____ home last Friday?
    A. did; go　　　　B. did; go to　　　　C. did; goes to　　　　D. did; goes

四、语言应用。(5小题，每题2分)

21. The picture means that you must _____.

    A. fasten safety belt
    B. loosen safety belt
    C. wear your shoes

22. If the original price is 130 RMB, now you need to pay _____ RMB.

    A. 130　　　　B. 32.5　　　　C. 97.5

23. If Jasmine gets a job offer, salary should be the _____ thing to consider.

    How to analyze an offer:
    1. Job's Daily responsibilities
    2. Career potential
    3. Learning potential
    4. Work environment
    5. Location
    6. Salary
    7. Intuitive impression

    A. sixth　　　　B. third　　　　C. first

— 1 —

24. According to the schedule, how many Chinese classes in a week?

Classes		Monday	Tuesday	Wednesday	Thursday	Friday
A.M.	First	Maths	Chinese	Chinese	Chinese	Maths
	Second	English	Maths practice	Calligraphy	P.E.	Art
	Third	P.E.	School based	English	Maths	English
	fourth	Chinese	Science	Maths	Music	Basket ball
P.M.	First	Ethics	Art	Chinese	English	Chinese
	Second	Class Meeting	Compositive Practice	Information technology	Ethics	Science
	Third	Peking Opera	Peking Opera	Peking Opera	Peking Opera	

  A. 4.   B. 5.   C. 6.

25. From the following picture, we know people choose _____ to work most.

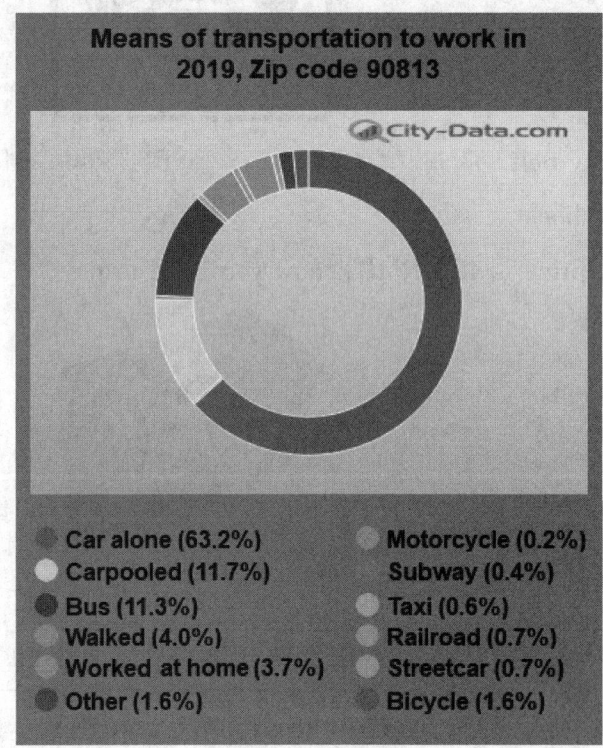

  A. car   B. carpool   C. bus

五、阅读理解。(15 小题，每题 2 分)

A

  The year 2022 will be a big year for sports in China. That's because it will hold not only the 24th Winter Olympic Games in Beijing, but also the 19th Asian Games in Hangzhou.

  On August 6, 2018, the official emblem(会徽) for the Hangzhou Asian Games came out. It will be the third Chinese city to hold the Asian Games after Beijing and Guangzhou in 1990 and 2010. Called "Surging Tides(潮汐)", the emblem includes six parts: a Chinese fan, the Qiantang River, a tidal bore(怒潮), a running track, the Internet icon and the glowing red sun of the Olympic Council of Asia(OCA).

  To make the Beijing Games a great success(成功), Chinese people worked hard to prepare. Beijing built a great number of roads and stadiums(体育场), including the famous National Olympic Sports Center and Olympic village.

  For the 2022 Asian Games, Hangzhou has already started building 33 sports venues(场馆). The themes(主题) for the Hangzhou Asian Games are "green, smart, economical and civilized".

26. The 24th Winter Olympic Games will be held in _____ according to the first paragraph.
  A. Hangzhou   B. Beijing   C. Guangzhou   D. Chengdu

27. Which city is the second one in China holding the Asian Games?
  A. Beijing.   B. Guangzhou.   C. Hangzhou.   D. China.

28. Which one is **TRUE**?
  A. The 19th Asian Games will be held in Guangzhou.
  B. Beijing built few roads and stadiums(体育场).
  C. The official emblem(会徽) for the Hangzhou Asian Games includes six parts.
  D. Hangzhou has already started building 30 sports venues(场馆).

29. National Olympic Sports Center was built for _____.
  A. Beijing Winter Olympic Games   B. Asian Games
  C. playing tennis   D. playing golf

30. The themes for the Hangzhou Asian Games are _____.
  A. green   B. smart
  C. economical and civilized   D. including A, B and C

B

  I am 15. Now I'm studying English in London. I want to invent a language machine that can help me understand as many languages as possible.

  Marie, France

  I am 13. I dream of going to a top university after I graduate. I want to be a reporter in the future.

  Michiko, Japan

I am a 12-year-old girl. I like traveling very much. How I wish to visit Egypt some day!

Masha, Russia

I am a 16-year-old girl in Tibet(西藏). The Qinghai-Tibet Railway has been built. I'll be able to reach Beijing by train in about 48 hours. My dream is to go to Beijing to watch the 2022 Winter Olympic Games.

Joma, China

I am 14 years old. I dream of inventing a machine that can send things or people from one place to another in a minute.

Andrew, the USA

31. What are they talking about?
    A. language   B. university
    C. traveling   D. their dreams
32. Who is Chinese?
    A. Andrew.   B. Masha.   C. Joma.   D. Michiko.
33. Marie is _____ years older than Masha.
    A. 4   B. 3   C. 2   D. 1
34. Where does Michiko come from?
    A. Japan.   B. China.   C. America. D. France.
35. Andrew want to invent a/an _____ that can send things or people very quickly.
    A. phone   B. rocket   C. car   D. machine

C

Water-Splashing Festival is the most ceremonious(浓重的) traditional festival of the Dai minority. It usually takes place in mid-April of the solar calendar, often ten days before or after the Tomb-sweeping Day, and lasts three to seven days. It is the New Year in the Dai calendar, and also a festival with the largest influence and maximum participating population among lots of minority festivals in Yunnan Province.

In the eye of the Dai People, water is a symbol of sanctity(神圣), beauty and brightness. So in this festival, people splash water each other for wishing luck, happiness and health. The more water one person is splashed, the more luck he/she receives, and the happier he/she will be. Besides water of splashing, there are lots of other conventions. Children will cut down bamboos to make squirt gun and play water game. People without reference to age and sex are all dressed up and climb up the mountain in groups to pick up flowers to make flower house.

36. The passage is about _____.
    A. tradition   B. festival   C. flower   D. water
37. Which Province do Dai People live in?
    A. Yunnan.   B. Sichuan.   C. Dai.   D. Guizhou.
38. How long will it last?
    A. 2 days.   B. About one week.
    C. 10 days.   D. 1 month.
39. What will people do according to the passage?
    A. Splash water.   B. Make squirt gun.
    C. Go shopping.   D. Both A and B.
40. What does "water" mean according to the passage?
    A. Wealth.   B. Sanctity.
    C. Coolness.   D. Kindness.

六、把左右栏相对应的句子匹配起来。（5小题，每题1分）

41. Merry Christmas, Bill!	A. for thousands of years.
42. Have you ever heard Mid-Autumn Festival?	B. the People's Republic of China was founded.
43. The Chinese have celebrated the Spring Festival.	C. Merry Christmas, Gina!
44. In 1949.	D. Yes, I have.
45. We have been good friends.	E. for 10 years.

七、英汉互译。（15小题，每题2分）

46. I want to invite you to a welcome party this Friday evening.
_____

47. It is a great game to get everyone to know each other better.
_____

48. We look forward to seeing you at this celebration.
_____

49. It is common for companies to hold an annual meeting around the New Year.
_____

50. Parties have become more and more popular in recent years.
_____

51. Li Lei needs a hand with all the preparation work.
_____

52. 班会将于5月10日晚上7点到8点举行。
There is _____ be a class meeting on May 10 th from 7 p. m. to 8 p. m.

53. 我喜欢在自助餐厅吃饭。
I like _____ in a _____.

54. 中国人庆祝春节。
Chinese people _____ the Spring Festival.

55. 我们期待着与您见面。
We are _____ to seeing you.

56. 这家店正在举行开幕仪式。
_____

57. 这对双胞胎有很多共同之处。
_____

58. 这个老板对员工很严厉。
_____

59. 公司将为新来的员工举办欢迎宴会。
_____

60. 我哥哥不在家。他去参加生日会了。
_____

Unit 6 单元测试

一、根据首字母或中文意思完成句子。(5 小题，每题 1 分)

1. The e_____ has become a very hot topic.
2. Hangzhou is f_____ for silk.
3. There are many _____(餐馆) near our school.
4. The q_____ of the clothes is very important.
5. The methods are many and v_____.

二、从方框中选择正确的短语并用正确的形式填空。(5 小题，每题 2 分)

| apart from   eat out   be able to   pay attention to   tend to |

6. Would you like to _____ with us?
7. _____ tears, only time could wear everything away.
8. We should _____ _____ _____ the cooking style.
9. Students _____ wear very little clothing for the same reason.
10. She _____ play the piano.

三、单项选择。(10 小题，每题 1 分)

11. The _____ on the tree turn green.
    A. leafes   B. leafs   C. leaf   D. leaves
12. We'd like to order three _____ of _____.
    A. cup; tea   B. cups; tea
    C. cup; teas   D. cups; teas
13. He _____ play football this afternoon.
    A. decides to   B. decide for
    C. decision to   D. decision for
14. There are many _____ we should consider when we choose a restaurant.
    A. factors   B. mushroom   C. feature   D. font
15. He likes to eat some _____ for lunch. It's very delicious.
    A. noodle   B. egg   C. beef   D. potato
16. My son _____ drinking milk in the morning.
    A. can't stand   B. take care of
    C. depend on   D. make a decision
17. Everyone should _____ to our society.
    A. contribute   B. contributes
    C. contribution   D. contributions
18. There _____ eight famous cuisines in China, offering various choices.
    A. be   B. is   C. are   D. am
19. _____ too much money on eating is unwise.
    A. Spend   B. Spending
    C. Spent   D. To spend
20. Would you like _____ to eat?
    A. nothing   B. anything   C. everything   D. something

四、语言应用。(5 小题，每题 2 分)

21. When we see the sign, we shouldn't _____.

    A. go straight   B. turn right   C. turn left

22. When can Lisa do business here?

    A. Any time on Monday.   B. 9:00 on Wednesday morning.
    C. 6:00 on Sunday evening.

— 1 —

23. Where are they?

A. At home. B. In the library. C. In the park.

24. It is a _____.

A. comedy B. cartoon C. talk show

25. Which course does Li Ming want to take?

A. An International English speaking course.

B. A certificate.

C. Talking with students from other countries.

五、阅读理解。(15 小题，每题 2 分)

A

FT Clothes Store		
Things	Colors	Price
Hat	Yellow, blue, black	¥7
Trousers	Black, blue, white, yellow	¥15
Socks	White, black	¥3
Sweater	Red, white, green	¥13
T-shirt	Blue, green, yellow	¥8

26. Which is the most expensive one?

A.  B.

C. 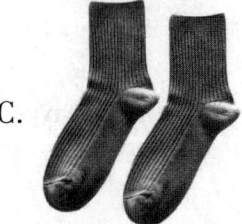 D.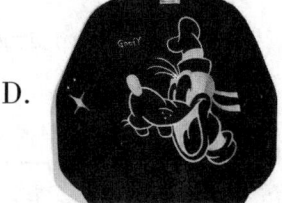

27. Two hats and a pair of socks are _____ yuan.

A. thirteen B. fourteen

C. seventeen D. twenty-nine

28. You can't buy _____ in FT Clothes Store.

A. green socks B. blue T-shirts

C. white trousers D. yellow hats

29. If you like black, and you have 10 yuan, you can buy _____.

A. a T-shirt B. a hat and a pair of socks

C. a sweater D. a pair of trousers

30. How many items are mentioned in the passage?
    A. Five.　　　　B. Four.　　　　C. Six.　　　　D. Seven.

B

Charlie is from the USA and he lives in Shenzhen. On Saturday, Tom goes there to see him with Mike and Ben. They take a train to go there. Charlie takes <u>them</u> to his home from the railway station. They have a party at Charlie's home. On Sunday, they go to a big clothes store. Tom always buys some clothes there. At about 5:00 in the afternoon, they are hungry, so they have dinner in a restaurant. After dinner, Tom, Mike and Ben take a train back to Zhuhai.

31. How many people are mentioned in the article?
    A. 3.　　　　B. 4.　　　　C. 5.　　　　D. 7.
32. How does Tom go to Shenzhen?
    A. By train.　　B. By bus.　　C. By car.　　D. By plane.
33. The underlined word them refers to _____.
    A. Mike and Ben　　　　　　B. Tom, Mike and Charlie
    C. Mike and Charlie　　　　D. Tom, Mike and Ben
34. Tom _____.
    A. is in China now　　　　　B. is in the USA now
    C. likes working on Saturday　　D. goes to work on Sunday
35. Which of the following statements is TRUE according to the passage?
    A. Tom is an English teacher.
    B. Charlie is from the UK.
    C. Mike lives in Zhuhai.
    D. Tom and Ben have lunch at Charlie's home on Sunday.

C

Healthy eating doesn't just mean what you eat, but how you eat. Here is some advice on healthy eating.

Eat with others. It can help you to see others' healthy eating habits. If you usually eat with your parents, you will find that the food you eat is more delicious.

Listen to your body. Ask yourself if you are really hungry. Have a glass of water to see if you are thirsty—sometimes you are just thirsty, you need no food. Stop eating before you feel full.

Eat breakfast. Breakfast is the most important meal of the day. After you don't eat for the past ten hours, your body needs food to get you going. You will be smarter after eating breakfast.

Eat healthy snacks like fruits, yogurt or cheese. We all need snacks sometimes. In fact, it's a good idea to eat two healthy snacks between your three meals. This doesn't mean that you can eat a bag of chips instead of a meal.

Don't eat dinner late. With our busy life, we always put off eating dinner until the last minute. Try to eat dinner at least 3 hours before you go to bed. This will give your body a chance to digest most of the food before you rest for the next 8-10 hours.

36. How much advice does the writer give us on healthy eating?
    A. 3.　　　　B. 4.　　　　C. 5.　　　　D. 6.
37. Which snack is Not mentioned in the passage?
    A. Fruits.　　B. Yogurt.　　C. Chips.　　D. Cheese.
38. Which is the most important meal of the day?
    A. Breakfast.　　B. Lunch.　　C. Dinner.　　D. Super
39. What does the underlined(画线) word "thirsty" means in Chinese?
    A. 口渴的.　　B. 饥饿的.　　C. 饱的.　　D. 酸的.
40. What is the topic of the passage?
    A. Where to Eat　　　　B. How to Eat
    C. Why to Eat　　　　　D. When to Eat

六、把左右栏相对应的句子匹配起来。(5小题，每题1分)

41. Can I take your order now?	A. Me too.
42. Anything to drink?	B. Yes, please.
43. I like fish and fruit salad.	C. I'd like some steak.
44. What would you like to eat?	D. Orange juice, please.
45. How would you like your steak cooked, rare medium or well-done?	E. Medium, please.

七、英汉互译。(15小题，每题2分)

46. Can I take your order now?
    _____

47. People with different backgrounds may like different tastes.
    _____

48. I invited my co-workers to have lunch together at home.
    _____

49. We should choose a restaurant within a proper price range.
    _____

50. Let's take a deeper look at food.

_____

51. Love me, love my dog.

_____

52. 世界上有不同的文化。

There are many different cultures _____ the _____.

53. 这家超市的服务相当好。

The _____ of this _____ is very good.

54. 鸡肉是今天的主食。

Chicken is our _____ today.

55. 此外，这家餐厅的菜看起来很棒。

_____, the dishes in the restaurant look good.

56. Tom 对中国食物很感兴趣。

_____

57. 川菜以辣出名。

_____

58. 我打算吃些面条。

_____

59. 熟能生巧。

_____

60. 好的服务可能会带给你更好的体验。

_____

Unit 7 单元测试

一、根据首字母或中文意思完成句子。(5小题,每题1分)

1. Excuse me. I'm doing a s_____ about online games.
2. Today, our mobile phones should not o_____ all of our time.
3. During a break, you log onto a _____(外卖的) app and order your favorite jiaozi.
4. You can use your mobile phone to _____(搜索) for a shared bicycle nearby.
5. Playing games online is quite p_____ among young people.

二、从方框中选择正确的短语并用正确的形式填空。(5小题,每题2分)

| log onto | have access to | do a survey | stay up | go over |

6. With this smart phone, you can _____ the Internet in a split second.
7. Mike _____ his lessons now because there's a test tomorrow.
8. _____ the take-out app and you can order your food.
9. It's really a bad habit to _____ playing computer games.
10. My roommate wants to _____ about online activities among teenagers.

三、单项选择。(10小题,每题1分)

11. It is _____ that more and more of the world's population will be living in cities.
    A. say   B. says   C. said   D. saying

12. — Could I use your bicycle?
    — _____ It's a spare one.
    A. Good idea.   B. Go ahead.
    C. No need.   D. You'd better not.

13. We have a lot of models for you to choose _____.
    A. from   B. to   C. for   D. with

14. —What activities do you usually do online?
    —I like _____ with my friends every day.
    A. sending   B. drinking   C. seeing   D. chatting

15. You should _____ your lessons carefully after class.
    A. go through   B. go for   C. go over   D. go after

16. It's really wise _____ before it's too late.
    A. to quit   B. to be quitted   C. to being quitted   D. quit

17. I couldn't even _____ on my studies.
    A. take   B. concentrate   C. spend   D. get

18. Many school students usually _____ late until midnight.
    A. put up   B. get up   C. look up   D. stay up

19. Be quiet, please. The baby _____ in the next room.
    A. sleeps   B. are sleeping
    C. is sleeping   D. was sleeping

20. Life in a smart city could be _____ safer, greener and more convenient.
    A. much   B. quite   C. lots of   D. well

四、语言应用。(5小题,每题2分)

21. The sign could be seen in a _____.

    A. restroom   B. dining-hall   C. classroom

22. The price of the first wine is _____ before discount.

A. $25　　　　B. $16　　　　C. $12

23. Customers will see the menu _____.

A. inside a restaurant　　　　B. on the table

C. outside a restaurant

24. This sign is on Tom's package, the delivery man should _____.

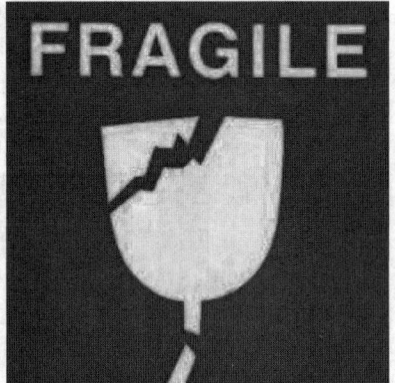

A. carry it gently　　　　B. carry it rudely

C. carry it carelessly

25. If you want to cross the street, what will you do first?

A. Cross the street directly.

B. Cross the street following others.

C. Push the button first.

五、阅读理解。(15 小题，每题 2 分)

A

You may know about "junk food" like French fries. But do you know about "junk sleep"?

Recently, a British survey found that electronic products(电子产品) in teenagers' bedrooms are affecting(影响) their sleep.

The survey was done among 1,000 British children from 12 to 16. It found that 30% of them got just 4 to 7 hours of sleep every day. But doctors say they need 8 to 9 hours.

Almost a quarter of the children said they fell asleep more than once a week while watching TV, listening to music or using other electronic products.

"This is very worrying." said Dr Chris, a British expert, "We call it 'junk sleep'. It means you don't get enough sleep and the quality of the sleep is bad, too. If you don't get good rest, you don't perform well in school the next day."

The survey found that 40% of the children felt tired each day, with girls between 13 and 16 feeling bad. Most of the teenagers have a phone, an iPad or TV in their bedrooms. And many of them have all three.

26. What is the main topic of this article?

　A. Junk food.　　　　　　　B. The importance of sleep.

　C. Electronic products.　　　D. Junk sleep.

27. _____ of the children in the survey fell asleep more than once a week while using electronic products.

　A. 100　　　　B. 150　　　　C. 200　　　　D. 250

28. "Junk food" and "junk sleep" are similar to each other in the way that _____.

　A. they are both low in quality

　B. they are both produced in factories

　C. people enjoy both in their spare time

　D. they are both good to people's health

29. Which of the following is NOT TRUE according to the passage?

　A. Teenagers need 8 to 9 hours of sleep each day.

　B. Most of the teenagers have a phone in their bedrooms.

　C. Girls between 15 and 16 spend the least time on electronic products.

D. Teenagers spend too much time on electronic products.

30. Which of the following is the best solution to the problem?

A. Parents watch TV together with their children.

B. Forbid teenagers to use any electronic product.

C. Teenagers limit(限制) their use of the electronic products.

D. The use of mobile phone and MP4 is not allowed at school.

B

Imagine one day on a weekend. Mr Li is at home alone. At 7:50, the phone reminds him of morning hobby classes. He will have lessons online. When he enters the online classroom, the teacher is talking about poems. He listens carefully, answers questions and discusses with classmates across the screen.

During a break, Mr Li logs onto a take-out app and orders his favorite jiaozi. It is sent to him at his desired time.

In the afternoon, he goes over the morning lessons. After sending homework to his teacher by email, he decides to have some fun. He clicks on a music app icon and chooses his favorite songs.

After an hour or so, Mr Li wants to go to the nearby park for some fresh air. While he puts on his shoes, his mobile phone is searching for the nearest shared bicycle to help him get on the move.

31. Where is Mr Li at 8:00 o'clock?

A. At school.   B. In the park.

C. At a restaurant.   D. At home.

32. What's the teacher talking about?

A. History.   B. English.   C. Poem.   D. Maths.

33. What's Mr Li's favorite food?

A. Jiaozi.   B. Beef steak.

C. Fried chicken.   D. French fries.

34. What will Mr Li do as soon as he goes over the morning lessons?

A. Going to the park.   B. Listening to music.

C. Sending homework to his teacher.   D. Ordering the food.

35. Which of the following could be the best title for the passage?

A. A Day with the Phone.   B. A Day with Mobile Internet.

C. A Day During the Holiday.   D. A Day Going Hiking.

C

Look around and you'll see many people busy on their smartphones. Smartphones do make our lives easier. But have you ever thought about what they mean to your eyes?

According to a recent study, 80% of British people own smartphones and they spend an average of two hours a day using them. There has been a 35% increase in the number of people in the UK who suffer from shortsightedness since smartphones were introduced there in 1997.

Staring at smartphones for a long time gives you dry eyes. When looking at something in the distance, your eyes automatically blink(眨眼) a certain number of times. However, when you look at things closer to your face, the blinking slows down. This reduces the amount of tears and causes discomfort in your eyes. Another bad habit is using smartphones in dark rooms before going to sleep. If you look at a bright screen when your pupils(瞳孔) become larger, too much light will enter your eyes. This can do harm to the eyes and cause a disease called glaucoma(青光眼).

While you're probably not going to stop using to your smartphone, there are a few things you can do to protect your eyes. Hold your phone at least 30 centimeters away from your eyes when using it. Take a break every hour and try the following: look at something at least five meters from you and then focus on the tip of your nose. Repeat this several times. It should reduce the discomfort in your eyes. So please remember to use your smartphones in a proper way.

36. The article is mainly about _____.

A. the rules to obey when using smartphones

B. the harm that smartphones do to users' eyes

C. the reason why teenagers get shortsightedness

D. advantages and disadvantages of smartphones

37. Since 1997, the number of people in the UK suffering from shortsightedness has increased by _____.

A. 80%   B. 2 hours

C. 35%   D. most of them

38. Using smartphones in dark rooms before going to sleep may cause _____.

A. too many blinks   B. more tears in the eyes

C. dry eyes   D. glaucoma

39. Which of the following is a proper way of using smartphones?

A. Use the phone for over an hour without a break.

B. Hold the phone at least 30 centimeters away from the eyes.

C. Turn off your phone for a couple of hours every day.

D. Use smartphones in dark rooms before going to sleep.

40. This article is written to advise people _____.

A. not to buy smartphones
B. to stop using smartphones
C. to make full use of smartphones
D. to use smartphones properly

六、把左右栏相对应的句子匹配起来。(5 小题，每题 1 分)

41. Hello sir, may I help you?	A. It's about 3,500 yuan.
42. What happened to John's old phone?	B. I'm thinking of buying a new phone.
43. How much is it?	C. Almost every day.
44. How often did you play?	D. OK, what would you like to ask?
45. Could you spare a few minutes?	E. It got slipped into the water.

七、英汉互译。(15 小题，每题 2 分)

46. This meal is a typical local specialty.
_____

47. A smart phone is a mobile phone that also has some of the functions of a computer.
_____

48. 5G network and the Internet of Things (IoT) are used widely.
_____

49. We are doing a survey about the smart city.
_____

50. You need a password to log onto the website.
_____

51. 在你的帮助下，我成功了。
_____ your help, I _____.

52. 快点！把外衣穿上！
Hurry up! _____ your coat _____!

53. 没有空桌子了。您愿不愿意与别人拼桌？
There isn't any _____ table available. Would you mind _____?

54. 多吃新鲜水果和蔬菜。
_____ plenty of _____ fruit and vegetables.

55. 请确保演出时所有手机处于关闭状态。
Please _____ all mobile phones are switched off during the performance.

56. 这是我最喜欢的电影之一。
_____

57. 我正在和我的同学上网课。
_____

58. 你能为我接个电话吗？
_____

59. 我曾玩过在线游戏。
_____

60. 你可以把手机当闹钟使用。
_____

Unit 8 单元测试

一、根据首字母或中文意思完成句子。(5小题，每题1分)

1. What's your favourite i_____?
2. The chief e_____ for this railway was Zhan Tianyou.
3. The Jingzhang Railway _____(延伸)from Beijing to Zhangjiakou.
4. I like the e_____ reader best.
5. It is considered a b_____ piece of work in Chinese railway history.

二、从方框中选择正确的短语并用正确的形式填空。(5小题，每题2分)

| ahead of schedule | return to | succeed in | show an interest in | stretch from |

6. Only by working hard can we _____ doing anything.
7. When did you first _____ tennis?
8. Let's _____ camp.
9. Thanks to your help, we accomplished the task _____.
10. The road _____ Guangzhou to Shenzhen.

三、单项选择。(10小题，每题1分)

11. There is _____ with my watch. It can't work.
    A. something wrong   B. anything wrong
    C. wrong something   D. nothing wrong
12. Susan plans _____ a talk next week.
    A. give   B. giving   C. to give   D. gives
13. —Can you speak Japanese?
    —No, I _____.
    A. mustn't   B. needn't   C. may not   D. can't
14. The children _____ play football on the road.
    A. can't   B. can   C. mustn't   D. must
15. —_____ you come to my birthday party tomorrow?
    —I'm afraid not. I _____ do my homework at home.
    A. Must; can   B. Can; must   C. Need; may   D. May; can
16. —Mrs. Zhou, Must I hand in my homework today?
    —No, you _____.
    A. mustn't   B. can't   C. shouldn't   D. needn't
17. They have _____ ideas.
    A. look of   B. run out of   C. take care of D. give up of
18. —_____ will you go to Beijing?
    —In about two weeks.
    A. How soon   B. How often   C. How long   D. How far
19. —Excuse me, where is the bank? —_____
    A. Sorry, I don't know.   B. I'm OK.
    C. I don't understand.   D. I can't miss it.
20. He has difficulty _____ up early.
    A. get   B. gets   C. getting   D. to get

四、语言应用。(5小题，每题2分)

21. How did Mr. Carl go to Shanghai yesterday?

    A. By air.   B. By ship.   C. By train.

22. What position is this for?

— 1 —

A. Engineer.　　　　B. Designer.　　　　C. Teacher.

23. What grade is this English book?

A. Grade one.　　　B. Grade two.　　　C. Grade three.

24. You can see the above sign in a _____.

A. public bathroom　　B. sitting room　　C. kitchen

25. You should _____ when you see the sign.

A. catch the vehicle　B. be very careful　C. turn around

五、阅读理解。(15 小题，每题 2 分)

A

Saturday, June 16th

In the morning, we went camping along a path in Green Natural Park. We were happy because it was a sunny day. We were expecting an enjoyable two-day holiday. On the way, we kept singing and making jokes.

However, in the afternoon, when we finished our picnic at one o'clock, it was dark and windy. Soon, there was a shower. Unluckily, none of us brought an umbrella. We ran about but we could find no place to hide.

Twenty minutes passed and it was still raining. There were hours to go before we reached the campsite (野营地). It was even worse that our small compass (指南针) showed that we went the wrong way. We had lost our way!

We had to make a quick decision as it was raining heavily. Chris said we could set up a tent to hide in, so Mary and Tom helped to set up the tent. Chris and I tried to make a fire to keep us warm. But we were unable to light the fire, for everything was wet. We dried ourselves, chatted and waited inside the tent. At about five o'clock, it stopped raining. We decided to give up the camping trip because all of us had been very tired.

This camping trip may not be very successful but we know each other better. And the most important thing I've learned from this trip is the importance of team spirit.

26. What month did the writer go camping in Green Natural Park?
　　A. In July.　　　B. In May.　　　C. In June.　　　D. In August.

27. It was even worse that they _____.
　　A. had no picnic　　　　　　　　B. lost their way
　　C. couldn't light the fire　　　　　D. couldn't know each other

28. Chris suggested that they should _____ in the rain.
　　A. set up a tent　　　　　　　　B. reach the campsite
　　C. keep singing　　　　　　　　D. find a place to hide

29. The writer has learned the importance of _____ from the trip.
　　A. making a decision　　　　　　B. working together
　　C. enjoying holidays　　　　　　D. taking a compass

30. Which of the following is TRUE?
　　A. It was rainy in the morning.
　　B. Everyone had an umbrella.
　　C. They gave up the camping at last.
　　D. They ran about to dry themselves.

B

Every living thing needs to reproduce. Reproducing means creating more members of your group. In order for plants to reproduce, they have to spread their seeds (种子) to other areas. Plants have developed all kinds of ways to do this.

The simplest way is gravity. Many seeds are inside of fruit. When a piece of fruit gets too heavy, it falls from a tree to the ground. Sometimes animals will pick up the fruit and drop it in another area. That helps move the seed even farther away. Apples spread this way.

Other plants use wind to spread their seeds. Dandelions are a good example of this. Dandelion seeds are so light that when wind blows, it carries dandelion seeds to new places. Maple(枫树) seeds also use wind. Their seeds are connected with long, thin leaves that look like wings. When the seed falls from the tree, its "wings" help it fly farther from the tree.

Some animals help plants spread their seeds. The animals eat the seeds. While the seed is in the animal's body, it stays whole. When the seed leaves the animal, it's in a new place.

Ants also help spread seeds. Some seeds have a special smell that attracts ants. The ants bring the seeds back to their home, which of course is underground. They only eat part of the seed. They leave the rest of the seed underground. After that, the seed can start growing.

31. What's the easiest way to reproduce?
    A. Wind.   B. Water.   C. Light.   D. Gravity.
32. How do maples spread their seeds?
    A. They use ants.   B. They use wind.
    C. They use smells   D. They use animals.
33. Which is not TRUE according to the last paragraph?
    A. Ants only eat part of the seed.
    B. Ants carry seeds to the underground home.
    C. Ants help seeds fall from the tree.
    D. They leave the rest of the seed underground.
34. What dose the article talk bout?
    A. Hobby.   B. Sport.   C. Culture.   D. Nature.
35. What's the best title for the text?
    A. How Plants Spread Seeds?
    B. Why Animals Pick Up Seeds?
    C. How Wind Helps Seeds Spread?
    D. Why Seeds Have a Special Trip?

C

Martin Strel is a swimmer, best known for swimming the world's big rivers. He was born in 1954. He taught himself to swim when he was six and became a professional(职业的) swimmer in 1978. Martin holds Guinness World Records for swimming the Danube River, the Mississippi River, the Yangtze River and the Amazon River.

Of all his achievements, the greatest is his Amazon River swim. The Amazon is known as the largest and most dangerous river in the world. Several swimmers had tried to swim it, but all failed. Martin wanted to show the world that people could achieve their dreams with hard work and perseverance(毅力).

On April 7th, 2007, Martin Strel completed his Amazon River swim all the way from Atalaya (Peru) to the Atlantic Ocean at Belem (Brazil). He struggled(奋战) with the river for 66 days and swam 3,274 miles in total.

People describe him as "Fishman" "Human Fish" or even "the Craziest Man in the World". In 2009, American filmmakers made a documentary called Big River Man. And the book, The Man Who Swam the Amazon, has been sold in many countries. It tells us an <u>inspirational</u> story of perseverance and hard work which has encouraged many people.

Martin doesn't swim for money. Instead, he swims teach people about the importance of keeping water clean.

Martin has always been looking for the challenges of the impossible. What is his next?

36. How did Martin learn to swim when he was young?
    A. By watching his partners.
    B. By learning from a coach.
    C. By teaching himself.
    D. By telling from friends.
37. What does the underlined word "inspirational" mean in and Paragraph 4?
    A. 鼓舞人心的。   B. 兴高采烈的。
    C. 栩栩如生的。   D. 心灰意冷的。
38. What is Martin's greatest achievement so far?
    A. Swimming the Nile River.
    B. Swimming the Amazon River.
    C. Swimming the Mississippi River.
    D. Swimming the Yangtze River.
39. According to the text, which is the goal of Martin swimming the big rivers?
    A. To make a lot of money for a good living.
    B. To be known by more people.
    C. To make exciting documentaries and best-selling books.
    D. To teach people the importance of keeping water clean.

40. What can be the best title (标题) of the text?
   A. Swim for Fun.
   B. Challenge the Impossible.
   C. Fight for Jobs.
   D. Break the Record.

六、把左右栏相对应的句子匹配起来。(5 小题，每题 1 分)

41. Can you pay for the dinner for me? I have no money with me.	A. He may eat less and do more sports.
42. He is getting fat.	B. Really?
43. There are lots of Chinese shops in New York.	C. No problem.
44. May I borrow your book?	D. Yes, of course.
45. Can I help you, madam?	E. I want two glasses of water.

七、英汉互译。(15 小题，每题 2 分)

46. Why do you like it most?
_____

47. I hope someday I can invent something useful.
_____

48. In recent years, China's high-speed trains have become faster and faster.
_____

49. He is very interested after hearing the interesting book.
_____

50. Do you believe his report?
_____

51. She overcame injury to win the Olympic gold medal.
_____

52. 祝你好运！
_____ have a good luck!

53. 我学习英语有困难。
I have _____ English.

54. 年轻人应该永远尊敬老年人。
_____ should always show _____ to old age.

55. She _____ her coat and went out.

56. 这篇文章给我们介绍了他的学习方法。
_____

57. 鸡蛋被认为是最有益于健康的食物之一。
_____

58. 另外，做家务也是一种锻炼。
_____

59. 我父母两个人都为我感到自豪。
_____

60. 它能帮助我们更加独立、更加负责。
_____

期中检测题

满分100分　考试时间120分钟

第Ⅰ卷(共两部分　满分70分)

第一部分　英语知识运用。(共两节；满分30分)

第一节　单项选择。(共15小题；每小题1分，满分15分)

从A、B、C、D四个选项中，选出可以填入空白处的最佳选项。

1. What _____ amazing film it is!
   A. a   B. an   C. the   D. /

2. The Mid-term examinations _____ next week.
   A. will take place   B. would take place
   C. takes place   D. took place

3. There is _____ milk in the fridge. I need to buy some.
   A. a few   B. few   C. a little   D. little

4. He _____ abroad for further studying for two years.
   A. has gone   B. have been   C. was   D. went

5. She was trying to solve the problem all by _____.
   A. her   B. herself   C. hers   D. she

6. _____ smoking in public places!
   A. Don't   B. Not   C. No   D. Can't

7. — _____ do you go to school every day? — On foot.
   A. Why   B. Where   C. How   D. Who

8. There is a box of _____ on the table.
   A. book   B. gift   C. cup   D. rice

9. I prefer _____ a bus to get home.
   A. taking   B. takes   C. took   D. take

10. This new edition adds _____ 1,000 new words.
    A. as many as   B. as much as   C. many   D. much

11. I think the price of the coat is so _____. So I won't buy it.
    A. expensive   B. cheap   C. high   D. low

12. This book _____ my major.
    A. relate   B. is related to
    C. is relates to   D. are related with

13. Hurry up! Our train _____ in ten minutes.
    A. is left   B. is leaving   C. has left   D. left

14. Many _____ are talking over there.
    A. woman teachers   B. women teacher
    C. woman teacher   D. women teachers

15. People often think they are _____ than they really are.
    A. even attractive   B. much attractive
    C. most attractive   D. more attractive

第二节　语言应用。(共10小题；每小题1.5分，满分15分)

Part A 根据下列图片所提供的信息，从16~22题所给的A、B、C三个选项中，选出最佳选项。

16. It's Thursday today. What's the date of Saturday?

Wednesday Jul 6	Thursday Jul 7	Friday Jul 8
☀ ☾	☀ ☾	☀ ☾
Sunny	Sunny	Sunny
High: 35 ℃	High: 35 ℃	High: 35 ℃
Low: 26 ℃	Low: 27 ℃	Low: 27 ℃
No wind	No wind	No wind

   A. July 9.   B. July 10.   C. July 11.

17. The sign means that _____.

   A. someone will welcome you when you enter the room
   B. you can enter the room if you are not authorized

— 1 —

C. you can enter the room if you are authorized

18. This picture aims to warn people _____ after drinking beer.

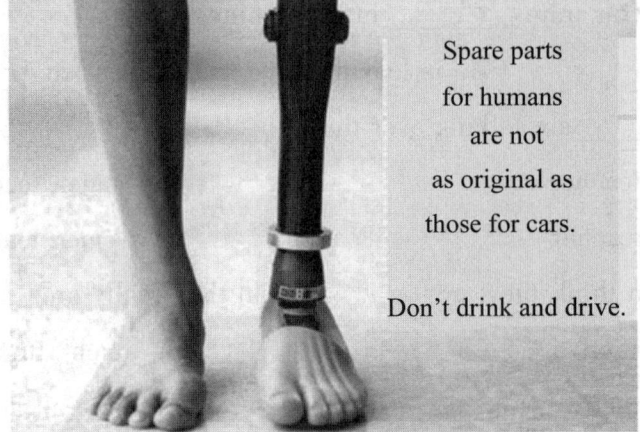

A. not to drive   B. to drive fast   C. to buy a car

19. When you see this sign, you should _____.

A. walk your dog every day

B. bring a dog with you if you want to have a walk

C. clean up after your dog poops

20. From the picture, we know that _____.

A. all visitors should report to the office

B. all visitors can come in freely without reporting

C. all visitors need to go back home to report

21. If you drink in this public places, you will be fined _____.

A. at most 500 pounds   B. at most 500 yuan

C. at least 500 dollars

22. What's the weather like on Sunday? It's _____.

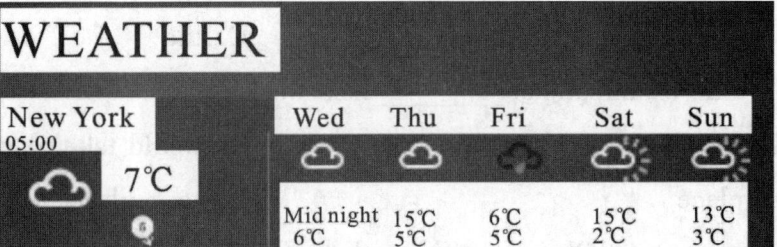

A. cloudy   B. rainy   C. sunny

Part B 根据下图所提供的信息，从 23~25 题所给的 A、B、C 三个选项中，选出最佳选项。

NOTICE
Mon-Fri 9:00—17:00
Sat-Sun 10:00—16:00
No Camera   No Pets
No Tossing   No Smoking

23. We can visit the museum _____.

A. at 9:30 on Sunday   B. at 10:30 on Sunday

C. at 17:00 on Saturday

24. You can visit the museum _____.

A. with your dog   B. at anytime every day

C. on Tuesday

25. When visiting the museum, you can _____.

A. smoke   B. throw rubbish everywhere

C. not take photos

第二部分　阅读理解。（5篇短文，共20小题；每小题2分，满分40分）

阅读下列短文，从每题所给的A、B、C、D四个选项中，选出最佳选项。

A

A kind of small car may take the place of big ones in no time. They will be popular. The car is as small as a bike. It can carry two people in it.

If everyone drives such a car in the future, there will be less pollution in the air. There will also be more space for cars and people in cities. Three such cars can fit in the space now needed for one car of the usual size.

These small cars will cost much less money to drive. They can only go 65 kilometers an hour. So driving will be safer, too. You can drive these cars to school or go around the city, but you'll better not use them for a long trip.

This kind of car can save a lot of gasoline(汽油). They can go 450 kilometers if they are *filled up*.

26. This passage is talking about _____.
    A. a save-energy vehicle　　　　B. a big car
    C. a bike　　　　D. a room

27. An usual size car can fit _____ such small cars according to the passage.
    A. one　　B. two　　C. three　　D. four

28. The underlined words "*filled up*" means _____.
    A. fast　　　　B. slow
    C. filled the car with gasoline　　D. the traffic

29. Which of the following is TRUE according to the passage?
    A. The small cars are not very popular in the future.
    B. Driving the small cars is very dangerous.
    C. The small cars cause no air pollution.
    D. The small car use less gasoline.

B

Dear editor,

I am a businessman who has been reading Modern China since 2015. Due to my work, I have travelled to many cities in China including Beijing, Shanghai, Xi'an, Guangzhou, and Shenzhen. My favorite one is Shanghai, which is the New York City of the East. I love the historic city of Xi'an too, which I have visited twice. Guangzhou is the manufacturing center and I am attracted by the delicious foods in this big city. Shenzhen, another city in southern China, feels similar to Los Angeles in California. For me, China is not that far apart as I read Chinese books and know many well-known Chinese people, for example, Father of Hybrid Rice Yuan Longping, the science fiction(科幻小说) writer Liu Cixin, and super star CoCo Lee.

Modern China is a window for me to learn more about China. Your stories about Chinese culture, people's life, current events, business, economics, history and politics are all interesting and attractive. All in all, Modern China is a high-quality magazine, but I think Modern China should also touch upon some issues or problems facing Chinese society. For example, environmental and economic problems can also be discussed so that foreigners can know what the real challenges are and what have been done or will be done to make a change. In this way, your magazine will provide more useful information and attract more readers.

Wesley Wilson
U.S.A.

30. What do we know about Wilson from the text?
    A. He is a reader of Modern China.　　B. He comes from Canada.
    C. He is an English teacher.　　D. He loves the Chinese countryside.

31. Which city is the New York city of the east according to Wilson?
    A. Shenzhen.　　　　B. Shanghai.
    C. Xi'an.　　　　D. Guangzhou.

32. From the letter, we know that "Modern China" is a _____.
    A. country　　　　B. magazine
    C. city　　　　D. famous people

33. Why did Wilson write this letter?
    A. To show his disappointment with the editor.
    B. To share his travelling experiences in China.
    C. To ask for more information about Modern China.
    D. To express his praise and suggestion for the magazine.

C

Traditionally, a person's 60th Birthday in China is seen as a very important point of life. Therefore, there is often a big celebration. After that, a birthday celebration is usually held every ten years, that is the 70th, the 80th, etc.

To make it grand, family members will invite relatives and friends to celebrate together. In Chinese culture, 60 years makes a cycle of a life. When one is 60 years old, he is expected to have a big family filled with children and grandchildren, which sometimes can be called "Four generations in one house (四世同堂)".

Peaches and noodles are popular. They mean "long life". But interestingly the peaches are not real. They are steamed bread with sweet stuff inside. Noodles should not be cut short, because the shortened noodles don't mean "long life".

Typical birthday presents are usually two or four of eggs, long noodles, artificial peaches, and money in red paper.

34. In order to make it grand, _____ will be invited to the 60th birthday celebration?
    A. only friends   B. friends and relatives
    C. family members   D. sons and daughters

35. The 60th birthday is seen as _____.
    A. a new life cycle's start B. the end of life
    C. the beginning of after-life D. the finishing of important celebration

36. All of the things below are used for birthday celebration EXCEPT _____.
    A. eggs   B. long noodles
    C. money in red paper   D. real peaches

37. Which is the best title for this passage?
    A. Birthday Celebration Customs.
    B. Four Generations in One House.
    C. The 60th Birthday, a Very Important Point of Life.
    D. Eggs, Noodles and Lucky Money in Red Paper.

D

Most college graduates wanted to find jobs in large cities. But Rui returned to her hometown, a small village in Changchun, to sell her home made bean curd (豆腐), shortly after she graduated from Changchun University in 2009.

Rui was the first woman in her big family to go to college. All her family were proud of her while she studied in the university. However, when she told them she would return home to make bean curd, to inherit (继承) the family business, most of them **turned a cold shoulder** to her. But Rui remembered her dream and followed her heart. She decided to use traditional methods to produce bean curd, in an effort to inherit the traditional cultural heritage (遗产) and promote the development of the traditional craft.

After she returned home in 2009, Rui turned her house into a plant. She and her family members made bean curd at night. Every day Rui got up at 3 a.m. and then carried heavy loads of bean curd to the market to sell the product. During the first month of her business, Rui lost 10 kilograms of body weight. However, because of Rui and her family's continuous efforts to improve the quality of the bean curd, her business grew rapidly.

Rui's efforts to develop her business have paid off, as the small plant has become a medium-sized food company. The company's bean products have sold well in many large supermarkets in Changchun. Her company is the only one in Changchun, whose hand made bean products have been given the National QS (quality standard) Certification.

38. Rui is from _____.
    A. Hebei Province   B. Jilin Province
    C. Hubei Province   D. Hainan Province

39. Rui started her business _____.
    A. when she was studying in university B. after her parents left
    C. after she quit her job   D. after she graduated from university

40. The underlined words "**turned a cold shoulder**" in para. 2 means _____.
    A. her family members are happy to her
    B. her family members are unsupported to her
    C. her family members are confused to her
    D. her family members are hopeful to her

41. What's the main idea of the passage?
    A. New Life to Traditional Bean Curd Craft.
    B. College Graduate and Her Bean Curd Business.
    C. College Students Back to Villages.
    D. Saving Traditional Cultural Heritage.

E

"Using a smartphone at mealtimes is making us fat," say scientists. Researchers have found that men and women took 15 percent more calories (卡路里) when looking at their phones while eating. They also ate more fatty food.

The study suggests that looking at a phone screen may distract(分散注意) people from how much food they are actually eating. "It may prevent the brain from correctly understanding the amount of food taken," said researchers who watched the volunteers eating alone. Sixty-two volunteers, men and women, aged 18 to 28, joined the study. *They* were invited to have different types of food—from healthy ones to soft drinks and chocolate—until they were satisfied. Only three of the volunteers were recorded eating with no distraction of a smartphone.

The volunteers ate 535 calories without the distraction of a smartphone but 616 when using a mobile. When using their mobiles, the volunteers also took 10 percent more fatty foods. "Smartphone user during a meal increased calorie and fat intake," said Marcio Gilberto Zangeronimoa, a lead author of the study—carried out at the Federal University of Lavras in Brazil and University Medical Center Utrecht in the Netherlands.

He added, "Smartphones have become the main dis-tractors during meals, even early in childhood. It's making us fat."

42. Researchers shows that using a smartphone took _____ more calories.
    A. 18%   B. 20%   C. 10%   D. 15%

43. What does the underlined word "*They*" in paragraph 2 refer to?
    A. Researchers.   B. Volunteers.
    C. Smartphones.   D. Drinks.

44. Volunteers without the distraction of smartphone ate _____ than those with it.
    A. less calories and less fatty foods   B. less calories but more fatty foods
    C. more calories and more fatty foods   D. more calories but less fatty foods

45. What's the purpose of the passage?
    A. Tell us "No More Fatty Foods".
    B. Tell us "Too Many Calories Do Harm".
    C. Tell us "Using Smart Phones While Eating Makes Us Fat".
    D. Tell us "Smartphones Hurt Our Brain".

第Ⅱ卷(共三节 满分30分)

第一节 补全对话。(共5小题；每小题1分，满分5分)

阅读下列对话，从所给选项中，选出能够完成对话的最佳选项，选项中有两个多余选项。

A: How many people are there in your family, Susan?
B: Four, my father, my mother, my brother and I. _____46_____
A: What does your father do?
B: _____47_____. He looks very kind, but sometimes he is strict with us.
A: _____48_____.
B: She is tall and nice, and _____49_____.
A: And your brother?
B: _____50_____, three years older than I am. He is a soldier.
A: Do you have any grandparents?
B: My grandpa is still living and very energetic. But he doesn't live with us.

A. He is a professor.
B. she work as a hotel manager.
C. We are getting on very well.
D. My school is beautiful.
E. How about your mother?
F. What about you?
G. He is twenty five.

46. _____ 47. _____ 48. _____ 49. _____ 50. _____

第二节 翻译。(共5小题；每小题2分，满分10分)

Part A 请将下面的英语句子翻译成汉语，并将答案写在相应的横线上。

51. Time is money!

_____

52. The course let us get some hands-on experience.

_____

53. Today, most people have digital cameras on their phones.

_____

Part B 请根据所给中文提示，将下列译成英语的句子补充完整，并把答案写在相应的横线上。

54. 学校生活不全都是学习。
    Life at school is _____ about study.

55. 这本书比那本书有趣多了。

— 5 —

This book is _____ interesting than that one.

第三节　书面表达。(满分15分)

Lucy 到新学校 2 个月了，她的朋友 Lily 写信询问她在职业学校的学习生活情况。请根据以下提示给 Lily 写一封回信。

提示：1. 职校生活很好，每天很忙，有许多课外活动；

2. 除了学习语、数、外等一些基础学科外，还要上一些专业课和实践操作课；

3. 新同学很友善，新老师要求严格，但很爱我们；

4. 我爱我的新学校，喜欢现在的学习生活。

Dear Lily,

　　I have received your letter. You want to know something about my school life. _____

_____

_____

_____

_____

_____

_____

_____

_____

Yours,
Lucy

期末检测题

满分 100 分　考试时间 120 分钟

第 I 卷(共两部分　满分 70 分)

第一部分　英语知识运用。(共两节；满分 30 分)

第一节　单项选择。(共 15 小题；每小题 1 分，满分 15 分)

1. The earth _____ around the sun.
   A. moves B. moved C. move D. moving

2. Mother's Day is coming, I am preparing a gift _____ her.
   A. of B. to C. for D. in

3. Don't _____ me, dad. I can take care of myself at school.
   A. think about B. talk about C. know about D. worry about

4. It _____ me two hours to clean my house yesterday.
   A. took B. to take C. take D. takes

5. —How much _____ the socks?
   —_____ 8 yuan.
   A. is; They're B. are; They're C. is; It's D. are; It's

6. Nowadays, many public places _____ people with free Wi-Fi in China.
   A. offer B. notice C. provide D. practice

7. Clothes made of cotton are usually _____ than those made of silk.
   A. cheap B. cheapest C. cheaper D. more cheap

8. We won't go hiking if it _____ tomorrow.
   A. rains B. rain C. will rain D. is raining

9. The company _____ a new supermarket next year.
   A. open B. is opening C. opens D. to open

10. She _____ this book for one week.
    A. have bought B. bought C. has bought D. has had

11. —What kind of _____ is it?
    —It is a kind of silk.
    A. experience B. material C. attendance D. invention

12. —Is the woman your English teacher?
    —It _____ be her. She has gong to the library.
    A. mustn't B. can't C. won't D. needn't

13. Hurry up, _____ you'll be late for school.
    A. or B. and C. so D. but

14. You'd better _____ the subway.
    A. to try B. trys C. trying D. try

15. _____ does he play basketball?
    A. How soon B. How far C. How often D. How long

第二节　语言应用。(共 10 小题；每小题 1.5 分，满分 15 分)

Part A　根据下列图片所提供的信息，从 16~22 小题所给的 A、B、C 三个选项中，选出最佳选项。

16. Which day is coming soon?

    A. Mother's Day.　B. Father's Day.　C. Teachers' Day.

17. Chenshan Shan is a(n) _____.

A. doctor B. sales manager C. engineer

18. You can learn _____ here.

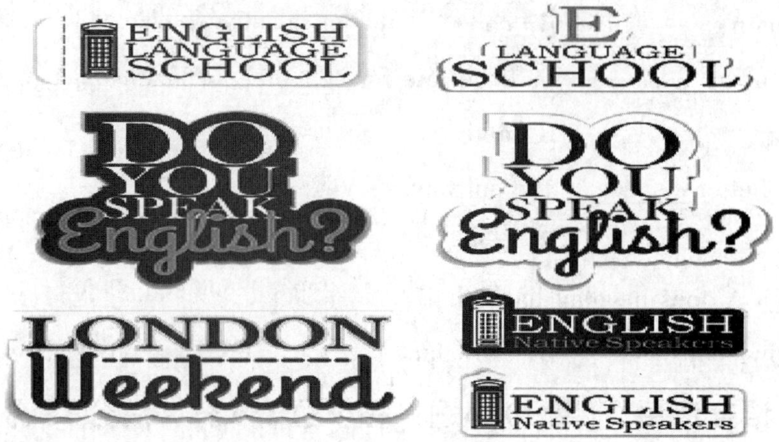

    A. English B. Maths C. Politics

19. When you see the sign, you should _____.

    A. turn left B. turn right C. stop

20. If you want to go to the restroom, you should _____.

    A. turn left B. turn right C. go straight

21. According to the picture, we can _____ here.

    A. rent bikes B. sell bikes C. buy bikes

22. The sign tells you that _____.

    A. you can leave from here
    B. you can get in from here
    C. you can enter from here

Part B 根据下列图片所提供的信息，从 23~25 小题所给的 A、B、C 三个选项中，选出最佳选项。

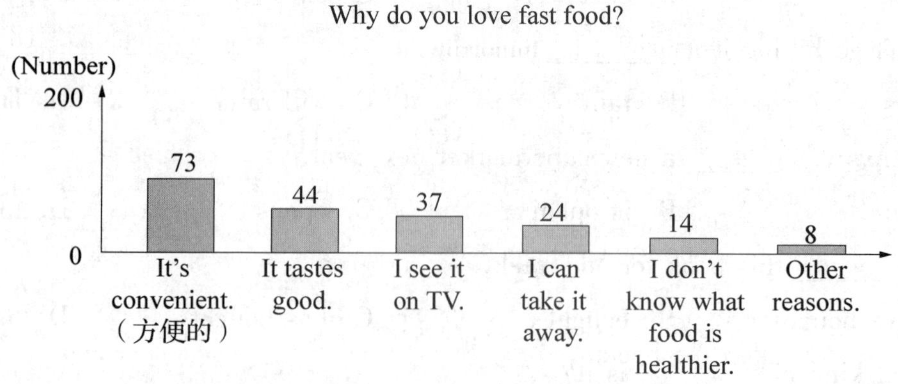

Why do you love fast food?

(Number)
200

73 — It's convenient. (方便的)
44 — It tastes good.
37 — I see it on TV.
24 — I can take it away.
14 — I don't know what food is healthier.
8 — Other reasons.

23. 44 people love fast food because it's _____.

    A. cheap B. delicious C. relaxing

— 2 —

24. The highest percentage of reasons for liking fast food is _____.

  A. quickly   B. healthy   C. convenient

25. How many people took part in the survey?

  A. 200   B. 73   C. 37

第二部分　阅读理解。(5 篇短文，共 20 小题；每小题 2 分，满分 40 分)

A

Eric is a sixteen-year-old boy now. Two years ago he came to the city and began to study in a middle school.

He studies hard and gets on well with his classmates. And he often helps his friends with their lessons. But as he comes from a village, the headmaster who was born in a rich family is bad to him and does his best to make excuses to punish him. The boy knows it and takes precautions against (提防) it. One afternoon all the students went to have lunch and he bought a piece of bread. He was reading a book under a big tree, while a dog was standing near him. At that moment the headmaster came out and saw it. He became angry and said,

"Don't you know we don't let anybody rear (饲养) dogs in the school?"

"Yes, I do, sir," said the boy.

"Why have you brought your dog to school, then?"

"It isn't my dog."

"Why is it following you, then?"

"You're following me now, sir," said the boy, "Can you say you are mine?"

26. How old is Eric now?

  A. 15.   B. 16.   C. 17.   D. 18.

27. Why did Eric come to the city two years ago?

  A. Because he studied in a middle school here.

  B. Because he wanted to make money.

  C. Because his parents worked in the city.

  D. Because he liked the headmaster.

28. Who is the owner of the dog?

  A. Eric   B. The headmaster.

  C. Tom's classmates.   D. We don't know.

29. Which of the following is TRUE?

  A. Eric comes from a village.

  B. The headmaster was born a poor family.

  C. The headmaster has a dog.

  D. Eric can't get on well with his classmates.

B

Do you know how to play a game called "Musical Chairs"? It is easy to play and most people enjoy it.

All you need are some chairs, some people and some ways of making music. You may use a piano or any other musical instrument, if someone can play it. You may use a tape recorder. You can even use a radio. Put the chairs in a row. The chairs may be put in twos, back to back. A better way is to have the chairs in one row with each chair facing in the opposite direction to the chair next to it. The game is easy. When the music starts, the players walk round the chairs. Everyone goes in the same direction, of course, they should walk in time to the music. If the music is fast they should walk quickly. If the music is slow, they should walk slowly. The person playing music cannot see the people in the game. When the music stops, the players try to sit on the chairs. If a person cannot find a chair to sit on, he drops out. Then, before the music starts again, one chair must be taken away. When the music stops again, one more player will be out. At last, there will be two players and one chair. The one who sits on the chair when the music stops is the winner.

30. If there are ten people want to play musical chairs, you must begin with _____.

  A. nine chairs   B. ten chairs   C. eleven chairs   D. one chair

31. If you play musical chairs with your classmates, you may not use _____.

  A. a guitar   B. a radio   C. a tape recorder   D. a cart

32. Which of the following statements is NOT true?

  A. The game "Musical Chairs" is not difficult to learn.

  B. The last one can sit on the last chair.

  C. The winner can sit on the chair.

  D. The players shouldn't walk in time to the music.

33. Which is the best title for this passage?

    A. How should we play a game?

    B. When should we play a game?

    C. Why should we play a game?

    D. Which game is the best?

C

    Mexico's neighbors are the United States to the north and Guatemala(危地马拉) and Belize(伯利兹城) to the south. Mexico is about one quarter of the size of the United States. Mexico has more than ninety million people. The language of Mexico is Spanish. This makes Mexico the worlds largest Spanish-speaking country.

    Mexico City is the capital and largest city of Mexico. The city is also very high. It is 7,349 feet high (2,240 meters). This makes it one of the highest capital cities in the world. The population, of Mexico City grows bigger every day. About thirty million people live there. It has more people than any other city in the world, even more than Tokyo.

    Mexico also has its specialities. Many of the foods we eat started in Mexico. Foods like beans, maize, avocados, tomatoes, peanuts, chili peppers, vanilla, and chocolate come from Mexico. Mexico is also famous for its cactus (仙人掌) plants. Mexico has more kinds of cactus than any other country.

34. The U.S.A is _____ Mexico.

    A. on the south of   B. on the north of

    C. a part of   D. as large as

35. Mexicans speak _____.

    A. English   C. French

    B. Spanish   D. Latin(拉丁语)

36. Which of the following is TRUE?

    A. Mexico City isn't the capital of Mexico.

    B. The population of Mexico City is about 30,000,000.

    C. Mexico is bigger than the U.S.A.

    D. Mexico City is the highest city in the world.

37. Beans were originally (最初) grown in _____.

    A. The U.S.A.   B. Spain   C. Tokyo   D. Mexico

D

    House fires often happened. So it appears necessary to learn something useful to protect family from them. The following poster in the neighborhood will tell you how to do it.

> Fire Safety
>
>   Put a smoke alarm in your house and test it every month. Half of all house fire deaths happen between 11 p.m. and 7 a.m. The risk of dying in a house fire is cut in half with working smoke alarms.
>
>   Make sure your <u>hearing aid</u>, wheelchair or eyeglasses are next to your bed. Fire can spread through a house soon. You may have as little as two minutes to escape(逃离) safely. Be ready to act at once.
>
>   Create a fire escape plan. 77% of families don't have a house fire escape plan to follow. That's one of the reasons why at least one child dies and 293 children are injured in a house fire every day.
>
>   Don't call 119 until you are safely outside. During a fire, the first thing to do is to get out of house as fast as you can.

38. What can make the risk of dying in a house fire smaller?

    A. A smoke alarm.   B. A pair of eyeglasses.

    C. A wheelchair.   D. A hearing aid.

39. If house fires are happened, we may have only _____ to escape from a house fire safely.

    A. half an hour   B. 2 minutes   C. 293 seconds   D. 2hours

40. What does the underlined(画线) word "hearing aid" means in Chinese?

    A. 眼镜   B. 钱包   C. 助听器   D. 手机

41. The purpose of the poster is to help people learn to _____.

    A. plan their live as they wish

    B. save time as much as possible

C. protect themselves in a right way

D. put a smoke alarm in their house

E

Recently I had a trip to Sydney with my parents. We visited the Wildlife Park.

The Wildlife Park has lots of different animals. Some are native(当地的) to Australia and can only be found there. There are more than 500 animals there, including kangaroos, koalas(考拉) and crocodiles(鳄鱼). They are kept in their natural environment. I like the Wildlife Park better than a zoo. In zoos, most of the animals are in cages(笼子).

We first spent some time with the kangaroos. We could touch and feel them. It was very exciting to be so close to them. There were koalas there too. They looked very cuddly(令人想拥抱的). Although we couldn't carry koalas, I could take a photo with one. It is a wonderful souvenir (纪念品) of my holiday in Sydney.

The Wildlife Park has plenty of freshwater crocodiles and saltwater crocodiles. Some of them are very big and scary(吓人的) with huge teeth! I did not want to get too close to them.

There was also a bird show. The keepers(饲养员) showed us different species(种类) of birds. I saw an old parrot(鹦鹉). It could "talk" and made a great impression on me.

I enjoy the trip very much. There was so much to see.

42. Where is the Wildlife Park?

　　A. In Australia.　　B. In Italy.　　C. In China.　　D. In Japan.

43. What is a wonderful souvenir of the writer's holiday?

　　A. A parrot that could talk.　　B. A chance to feed a koala.

　　C. A photo with a koala.　　D. Food for the kangaroos.

44. Which of the following statements is NOT true?

　　A. In the Wildlife park, most of the animals are in cages.

　　B. The writer visited the kangaroos first.

　　C. The writer loved the trip.

　　D. We can carry koalas.

45. After visiting the Wildlife Park, the writer felt _____.

　　A. bored　　B. upset　　C. excited　　D. homeless

第Ⅱ卷(共三节 满分30分)

第一节 补全对话。(共5小题；每小题1分，满分5分)

阅读下列对话，从所给选项中，选出能够完成对话的最佳选项，选项中有两个多余选项。

A：Hello! _____46_____

B：I'd like a pair of shoes, please.

A：How about these? They are very popular.

B：I like the style. Can I try them on?

A：Of course. _____47_____

B：32.

A：Here you are. The fitting room is over there.

B：It fits well. _____48_____

A：160 yuan. They are on sale now.

B：Good. _____49_____ Can I pay with my smart phone?

A：Sure. _____50_____

B：Here.

A：Thank you very much.

```
A. Can I help you?
B. Please show me your payment code.
C. Why do you like them?
D. How can I pay for them?
E. How much are they?
F. I'll take them.
G. What size are you?
```

46. _____　47. _____　48. _____　49. _____　50. _____

第二节 翻译。(共5小题；每小题2分，满分10分)

Part A 请将下面的英语句子翻译成汉语。

51. I live with my parents and my younger sister.

52. I'm doing a survey about online games.

_____

53. Seeing is believing.

_____

Part B 请根据所给中文提示，将下列译成英语的句子补充完整。

54. 毕业后，他放弃了大城市里的工作，回到了家乡。

   He _____ _____ a job in a big city and came back to his hometown after graduation.

55. 我能利用它做很多事情，比如和朋友们聊天和自拍。

   I can do a lot of things with it, _____ _____ chatting with friends and taking selfies.

第三节 书面表达。（满分 15 分）

请根据下面信息提示，写一篇 80 词左右的短文，向你的同学介绍你自己。

李华，男，16 岁，来自达州，是华兴职业学校的一名学生。

最喜欢的科目是英语和数学；擅长踢足球，会弹吉他。

喜欢看书、听音乐和爸爸一起打电脑游戏。

爸爸是一名工程师，妈妈是一名医生。

电话号码：2355896

参考词汇：vocational school，be good at，computer games，guitar

参考答案

Unit 1 单元测试

一、根据首字母或中文意思完成句子。(5小题,每题1分)

1. (f)amily 2. (m)anager 3. energetic 4. (e)specially 5. community

二、从方框中选择正确的短语并用正确的形式填空(5小题,每题2分)

6. vocational 7. are strict with 8. visits 9. introduce 10. cooking

三、单项选择。(10小题,每题1分)

11-15 CBADB   16-20 ACADB

四、语言应用。(5小题,每题2分)

21-25 CABCA

五、阅读理解。(15小题,每题2分)

26-30 ABCDB   31-35 ABDBC   36-40 BABCD

六、把左右栏相对应的句子匹配起来。(5小题,每题1分)

41-45 DCAEB

七、英汉互译。(15小题,每题2分)

46. 让我告诉你一些关于我家庭的事。

47. 站在我父亲旁边的那个男孩是我的弟弟。

48. 我的英语老师经常帮助我学习英语。

49. 我父亲正在为我妹妹准备一架手工制作的飞机。

50. 太阳东升西落。

51. 鲁是他母亲的姓,迅的意思是快。

52. strict;with

53. go;jogging

54. plan;to

55. pay;attention

56. By the way;where are you from?

57. This little boy must be you.

58. Chongyang Festival is coming.

59. We often go to school by bus.

60. He lives alone in a big house.

Unit 2 单元测试

一、根据首字母或中文意思完成句子。(5小题,每题1分)

1. (h)ire 2. (p)rovince 3. (c)onvenient 4. (a)ddress 5. habits

二、从方框中选择正确的短语并用正确的形式填空。(5小题,每题2分)

6. be late for 7. shuttle bus 8. worry about 9. on the right 10. rush hour

三、单项选择。(10小题,每题1分)

11-15 DBBCA   16-20 ADCDC

四、语言应用。(5小题,每题2分)

21-25 BACAC

五、阅读理解。(15小题,每题2分)

26-30 DBAAC   31-35 BDCBA   36-40 BDCCB

六、把左右相对应的句子匹配起来。(5小题,每题1分)

41-45 CBEAD

七、英汉互译。(15小题,每题2份)

46. 这个周末我没有太多家庭作业需要做。

47. 这是我们继续下去的动力。

48. 你应该在晚上9点以前搭乘班车。

49. 在下一个公交车站有许多共享单车。

50. 比起去购物我更喜欢待在家。

51. 早点起床，你就可以赶上早班车。

52. take; get to

53. How long

54. There is

55. opposite to

56. Go along the road and turn right at the first crossroads.

57. Could you tell me the way to the Summer Palace?

58. Change for Subway Line 3 at Zhonghua station.

59. Would you like to go by bus or by subway?

60. I'm thinking of taking a taxi.

Unit 3 单元测试

一、根据首字母或中文意思完成句子。(5小题，每题1分)

1. (t)raditional   2. (o)nline   3. bestselling   4. (b)etter   5. (s)maller

二、从方框中选择正确的短语并用正确的形式填空。(5小题，每题2分)

6. pay with   7. is good for   8. are rich in   9. on sale   10. fitting room

三、单项选择。(10小题，每题1分)

11-15 DACBA   16-20 DBCDC

四、语言应用。(5小题，每题2分)

21-25 CBAAB

五、阅读理解。(15小题，每题2分)

26-30 DDCAA   31-35 BAABD   36-40 CDABC

六、把左右栏相对应的句子匹配起来。(5小题，每题1分)

41-45 CBEAD

七、英汉互译。(15小题，每题2分)

46. 互联网正在改变我们的购物方式。

47. "双11"是中国最著名的网络购物日之一。

48. 越来越多的人开始享受网购。

49. 棉布做的衣服通常比丝绸做的便宜。

50. 三加一等于多少？

51. 这种书卖得很好。

52. work out

53. How much

54. made of

55. more; better

56. Please explain the article in English.

57. He wrote many bestselling novels.

58. Good communication is important.

59. He is taller than any other student in his class.

60. The list includes many new names.

Unit 4 单元测试

一、根据首字母或中文意思完成句子。(5小题，每题1分)

1. (s)killed   2. (h)old   3. (P)ractice   4. (e)xciting   5. (f)avorite

二、从方框中选择正确的短语并用正确的形式填空。(5小题，每题2分)

6. are over   7. all kinds of   8. different from   9. sounds like   10. take part in

三、单项选择。(10小题，每题1分)

11-15 CACAB   16-20 ABCBD

四、语言应用。(5小题，每题2分)

21-25 CABAA

五、阅读理解。(15小题，每题2分)

26-30 DDDCD   31-35 CABAD   36-40 CACAA

六、把左右栏相对应的句子匹配起来。(5小题，每题1分)

41-45 CEBAD

七、英汉互译。(15小题，每题2分)

46. 我喜欢计算机，但它不是我的最爱。

47. 我认为英语实用又有趣。

48. 放学后我们可以一起走吗？

49. 他们明天将在哪儿野餐？

50. 我可以完成工作后，去为会议做些准备。

51. 做一些有乐趣的事能让我们放松且有助于学习。

52. take part in

53. make; for

54. development; new products

55. pay special attention

56. You should not spend too much tome on playing online games.

57. It sounds like vocational high schools are not different from normal high schools.

58. Doing internships at real companies is a great way to learn skills.

59. I will graduate from Guanghua Vocational School next year.

60. We will take the final exams from July 6th to July 10th.

Unit 5 单元测试

一、根据首字母或中文意思完成句子。(5小题，每题1分)

1. (b)anquet   2. (f)orward   3. ideas/advice/suggestions   4. (r)ole   5. (h)elp

二、从方框中选择正确的短语并用正确的形式填空。(5小题，每题2分)

6. on behalf of   7. opening ceremony   8. play an important role in

9. helps with   10. in common

三、单项选择。(10小题，每题1分)

11-15 BCCAD   16-20 CCACA

四、语言应用。(5小题，每题2分)

21-25   ACCCA

五、阅读理解。(15小题，每题2分)

26-30 BBCAD   31-35 DCBAD   36-40 BABDB

六、把左右栏相对应的句子匹配起来。(5小题，每题1分)

41-45 CDABE

七、英汉互译。(15小题，每题2分)

46. 我想邀请你这周星期五晚上来参加欢迎宴会。

47. 这是一个极好的游戏，人们可以彼此更好地认识。

48. 我们期待在庆祝会上见面。

49. 每年新年前后，公司举办年终大会是很常见的。

50. 近些年，聚会(派对)变得越来越流行。

51. 李雷需要帮忙，帮他一起做所有的准备工作。

52. going to

53. eating; cafeteria

54. celebrate

55. looking; forward

56. The new shop is having/holding an opening ceremony.

57. The twins have a lot in common.

58. The boss treats strictly to his employees. /This boss is strict with his employees.

59. The company will have/hold/throw a welcome banquet for the new employees.

60. My brother isn't at home. He has gone to the birthday party.

Unit 6 单元测试

一、根据首字母或中文意思完成句子。(5小题，每题1分)

1. (e)nvironment   2. (f)amous   3. restaurants   4. (q)uality   5. (v)arious

二、从方框中选择正确的短语并用正确的形式填空。(5小题，每题2分)

6. eat out   7. Apart from   8. pay attention to   9. tend to   10. is able to

三、单项选择。(10小题，每题1分)

11-15 DBAAC   16-20 AACBD

四、语言应用。(5小题，每题2分)

21-25 BBCAA

五、阅读理解。(15小题，每题2分)

26-30 DCABA   31-35 BADAC   36-40 CCAAB

六、把左右栏相对应的句子匹配起来。(5小题，每题1分)

41-45 BDACE

七、英汉互译。(15小题，每题2分)

46. 请问你要点菜了吗？

47. 不同背景的人喜欢的口味可能不同。

48. 我邀请了我的同事们一起在家吃午饭。

49. 我们应该选择价格区间合适的餐馆。

50. 让我们更深入地了解食物。

51. 爱屋及乌。

52. in; world

53. service; supermarket

54. main course

55. In addition

56. Tom is very interested in Chinese food.

57. Sichuan Cuisine is known for being spicy.

58. I am going to eat some noodles.

59. Practice makes perfect.

60. Good service may give you a better experience.

Unit 7　单元测试

一、根据首字母或中文意思完成句子。(5小题，每题1分)

1. (s)urvey   2. (o)ccupy   3. take-out   4. search   5. (p)opular

二、从方框中选择正确的短语并用正确的形式填空。(5小题，每题2分)

6. have access to   7. is going over   8. Log onto   9. stay up   10. do a survey

三、单项选择。(10小题，每题1分)

11-15 CBADC   16-20 ABDCA

四、语言应用。(5小题，每题2分)

21-25 ABCAC

五、阅读理解。(15小题，每题2分)

26-30 DDACC   31-35 DCACB   36-40 BCDBD

六、把左右栏相对应的句子匹配起来。(5小题，每题1分)

41-45 BEACD

七、英汉互译。(15小题，每题2分)

46. 这是当地典型的特色菜。

47. 智能手机是一种兼有某些计算机功能的手机。

48. 5G网络和物联网被广泛使用。

49. 我们正在做一个关于智慧城市的调研。

50. 登录网站需要密码。

51. With; succeed

52. Put; on

53. empty; sharing

54. Eat; fresh

55. make; sure

56. It's one of my favorite movies.

— 4 —

57. I'm having online classes with my classmates now.

58. Can you answer the phone for me?

59. I used to play online games.

60. You can use a mobile phone as a clock alarm.

Unit 8 单元测试

一、根据首字母或中文意思完成句子。(5 小题，每题 1 分)

1. (i)nvention   2. (e)ngineer   3. stretches   4. (e)book   5. (b)rillant

二、从方框中选择正确的短语并用正确的形式填空。(5 小题，每题 2 分)

6. succeed in   7. show an interest in   8. return to   9. ahead of schedule

10. stretches from

三、单选。(10 小题，每题 1 分)

11-15 ACDCB   16-20 DBAAC

四、语言应用。(5 小题，每题 2 分)

21-25 CBAAB

五、阅读理解。(15 小题，每题 2 分)

26-30 CBABC   31-35 DBCDA   36-40 CABDB

六、把左右栏相对应的句子匹配起来。(5 小题，每题 1 分)

41-45 CABDE

七、英汉互译。(15 小题，每题 2 分)

46. 你为什么最喜欢它？

47. 希望有一天我也能发明有用的东西。

48. 近年来，中国的高铁速度已经越来越快。

49. 听了那本有趣的书之后，他很感兴趣。

50. 你相信他的报告吗？

51. 她战胜了伤痛，赢得了奥运会金牌。

52. Wish；you

53. difficulty；learning

54. Youth；respect

55. put；on

56. This article introduces us his studying method.

57. Eggs are supposed to be one of the most healthful foods.

58. Besides, doing housework is also a kind of exercise.

59. Both of my parents feel proud of me.

60. It can help us to be more independent and be more responsible.

期中检测题

第Ⅰ卷(共两部分 满分 70 分)

第一部分　英语知识运用。(共两节；满分 30 分)

第一节　单项选择。(共 15 小题；每小题 1 分，满分 15 分)

1-5 BADAB   6-10 CCDAA   11-15 CBBDD

第二节　语言应用。(共 10 小题；每小题 1.5 分，满分 15 分)

16-20 ACACA   21-25 ACBCC

第二部分　阅读理解。(共 20 小题；每小题 2 分，满分 40 分)

26-30 ACCDA   31-35 BBDBA

36-40 DCBDB   41-45 BDBAC

第Ⅱ卷(共三节 满分 30 分)

第一节　补全对话。(共 5 小题；每小题 1 分，满分 5 分)

46-50 CAEBG

第二节　英汉互译。(共 5 小题；每小题 2 分，满分 10 分)

51. 时间就是金钱。

52. 这个课程让我们获得了一些实际操作的经验。

— 5 —

53. 如今，许多人的手机上都带有数码相机。

54. not all

55. much more

第三节　书面表达。(满分 15 分)

参考范文：

Dear Lily,

　　I have received your letter. You want to know something about my school life. I came into a vocational school after leaving the junior middle school. We learn both some basic subjects such as Chinese, maths and English and some practice training courses. We are busy every day. We also have all kinds of activities to choose from in this school. I think my school life is wonderful. The teachers in this school are strict with us but they love us very much. Besides, my classmates are all very kind and helpful, we get on well with each other. I love my new school and enjoy my school life.

期末检测题

第Ⅰ卷(共两部分　满分 70 分)

第一部分　英语知识运用。(共两节；满分 30 分)

第一节　单项选择。(共 15 小题；每小题 1 分，满分 15 分)

1-5 ACDAB　　　　6-10 CCABD　　　　11-15 BBADC

第二节　语言应用。(共 10 小题；每小题 1.5 分，满分 15 分)

16-20 ABACB　　　21-25 AABCA

第二部分　阅读理解。(共 20 小题；每小题 2 分，满分 40 分)

26-30 BADAA　　　31-35 DDABB

36-40 BDABC　　　41-45 CACAC

第Ⅱ卷(共三节　满分 30 分)

第一节　补全对话。(共 5 小题；每小题 1 分，满分 5 分)

46-50 AGEFB

第二节　英汉互译。(共 5 小题；每小题 2 分，满分 10 分)

51. 我和父母还有妹妹住在一起。

52. 我正在做一个关于网络游戏的调研。

53. 眼见为实。

54. gave up　　66. such as

第三节　书面表达。(满分 15 分)

　　Hello, everyone! My name is Li Hua. I am 16 years old. I come from Dazhou. It's a beautiful city. I am a student in Hua Xing Vocational School. English and maths are my favorite subjects. I am good at playing soccer and I can play the guitar well. I like reading and listening to music. At the same time, I like playing computer games with my father. My father is an engineer. My mother is a doctor. My telephone number is 2355896. That's all, thank you very much.